REVITALIZE YOUR PRAYER LIFE

INSPIRED LIVING SERIES COMPANION

REVITALIZE YOUR PRAYER LIFE

*Rush into God's Presence
Put an End to Devotional Boredom*

BY
CECIL MURPHEY
New York Times Bestselling Author

Copyright © 2013 Cecil Murphey.
Original version published in 1997 as Invading the Privacy of God.

All Scripture quotations are taken from the Holy Bible, New Living Translation, copyright 1996, 2004, 2007 by Tyndale House Foundation. Used by permission of Tyndale House Publishers, Inc., Carol Stream, Illinois 60188, USA. All rights reserved.

Scripture quotations marked NIV are taken from the Holy Bible, New International Version ®, NIV®. Copyright © 1973, 1978, 1984, 2011 by Biblica, Inc.™ Used by permission of Zondervan. All rights reserved worldwide. www.Zondervan.com

Scripture taken from the New King James Version. Copyright © 1979, 1980, 1982, by Thomas Nelson, Inc. Used by permission. All rights reserved.

No part of this book may be reproduced in any form or by any electronic or mechanical means including information storage and retrieval systems, without permission in writing from the author. The only exception is by a reviewer, who may quote short excerpts in a review.

Cover Photo by Jeff Pang.

eISBN: 978-1-937776-58-9
ISBN: 978-1-937776-86-2

Other Books by Cecil Murphey

Inspired Living Devotional Series:

Devotions for Couples
Devotions for Dieters
Devotions for Runners
Revitalize Your Prayer Life: Inspired
Living Series Companion

More Titles:

90 Minutes in Heaven (with Don Piper)
Gifted Hands: The Ben Carson
Story (with Dr. Ben Carson)
Rebel with a Cause (with Franklin Graham)
Because You Care: Spiritual Encouragement for
Caregivers (by Cecil Murphey and Twila Belk)
When Someone You Love No Longer Remembers
The Spirit of Christmas (by Cecil
Murphey and Marley Gibson)
Unleash the Writer Within
Knowing God, Knowing Myself
When a Man You Love Was Abused
When God Turned Off the Lights

INTRODUCTION

Prayer bores me and I sometimes wonder why I'm doing it. *There!* I said it in print. Now anyone in the world can know about my problem with prayer.

Yet prayer also excites me and enables me to sense the loving presence of God. That's the other side of my experience with prayer.

That's how I spoke about prayer 15 years ago. I've since revitalized my prayer life and want to share my good news with others.

Dating back to my conversion to the Christian faith when I was in my early twenties, I have vacillated between those two extremes: being excited about prayer and being bored by it. I've read dozens of books on the subject; learned four different methods for praying the Lord's Prayer; embraced techniques for praying the Psalms; recited the Jesus Prayer ("Lord Jesus Christ, be merciful to me, a sinner") for nearly an hour at a time; taken lessons on meditation techniques; praised my way out of despair; sung hymns of petition; and like a lot of others, I've used the Adoration, Confession,

Thanksgiving, and Supplication (ACTS) method of prayer.

Did those methods work? Yes, all of them worked for me—sometimes and for a while. I've experienced moments when I prayed and felt such a closeness to Jesus Christ that it seemed I could actually feel a hand wrap itself around mine.

Those were the best of times. At the worst of times, I've fallen asleep on my knees, or I've prayed for four minutes that felt like two hours. I've tried to pray when my mind refused to disengage from distractions and I found myself constantly returning to the six other things I preferred to do at that moment.

Does this sound like your experience?

Prayer is a personal and, most of the time, private matter, which makes it subjective. When I pray, it reflects how I feel right then, at that moment. I've not always accepted the fact that sometimes I just don't feel like praying. Instead, I've upbraided myself for my lack of concentration or absence of emotion. "Pray no matter how you feel," I've commanded my soul. "Get past your boredom. Rally yourself. Press onward!"

I've said the words, but usually they haven't done much good. They haven't made prayer any more meaningful. The self-exhortations only increased my guilt level.

I've accepted the reality that I'll never learn the perfect method for praying the perfect prayer—the one where I know I'm in the presence of God, I know the Spirit is hearing me, and I can sense that the answers have already begun to swoop toward earth. But I believe in prayer, and it has remained a significant discipline of my life.

I don't have all the answers about how to pray, but I have found out something I didn't understand before. The most significant lesson I learned was to focus on God and not on Cec Murphey.

Obvious? Perhaps to many, but not to me. I concentrated on what I wanted or felt I needed. Of course I always, always made sure I intoned "according to your will" or something similar.

I also asked one question: What is *the* right way to pray? I wanted to figure out the exact formula for a vital, exciting relationship with God.

One day I thought about the way I prayed. It occurred to me that I directed most of my prayers to my heavenly Father, sometimes to the Holy Spirit, and occasionally it was Lord Jesus.

Then I realized that my approach to prayer was extremely limited. God is more than just my heavenly Father (and that's not to minimize the concept). As multi-faceted as God is, there was no way I could know him totally. At best, I could perceive only one part of God's personality at any one time.

Those thoughts made me remember the first time I saw the Lincoln Memorial in Washington, DC. When I faced the nineteen-foot statue of the great president directly from the front, I felt overwhelmed at the size of the figure. His eyes seemed to bore into mine.

When I walked to one side, though, my viewpoint changed. Although it was still an awesome statue, his eyes no longer overwhelmed me. I moved to the other side and envisioned how he would look when he laughed and told one of his famous stories. Each time I changed my position, I saw a slightly different version of the statue.

When I was leaving the monument, I stopped at the bottom of the steps and turned back. Lincoln didn't seem so foreboding, so serious, or so powerful.

Recalling that experience, a beam of light whirled inside my head. *I understood.* The statue of Lincoln never altered; the difference was in my viewpoint. In the same way, God is the Unchanging One, yet multifaceted; God is the All-Powerful Being, yet full of grace.

When I talk to God, I may see one facet of the divine personality until I refocus my thinking and perceive another. I'll never know everything there is to know about our great and mighty God, but I can continue to grow in my ability to perceive who God is. I can come to God in different ways: as my Father, my Savior, my Creator, my Master, the One Who Lives Within, my closest Friend, or my Defense Counsel.

As I understand the many facets of God better, I'll improve my understanding of how to pray.

As I focused on the many approaches we can take to God, I entered into a new adventure in prayer.

I figured out the answer to *the* right way to pray. It's simple: There is no one method of prayer. We can approach God in many ways. As obvious as that may be to many, it was startling to me. As a result, my inner life began to change dramatically that day. I realized I could truly come to God in a hundred different ways and still never exhaust them all.

This book is about my personal journey into prayer. Here are my experiences and attempts to make prayer relevant and meaningful in day-to-day encounters with God. As I share my discoveries with you, will you come with me and explore the many facets of God's personality? Will you learn with me about the wondrous attributes of God who is both unknowable and yet continually self-revealing through the Bible and the world in which we live?

> Ask me and I will tell you remarkable
> secrets you do not know about things
> to come (Jeremiah 33:3).

God, you are unknowable and fully
beyond our understanding.
Yet you choose to reveal yourself to us.
Help me grasp more of who you are. Teach me about your
Holy Self as I learn about myself and my world. Amen.

Chapter One
The Awesome God

When I was in grade school, our class visited the planetarium. In a darkened room, we stared upward at the ceiling. Tiny sparks of light twinkled and the objects slowly rotated. "This is the heavens," the guide's voice said. "These are stars and planets millions and millions of miles away."

He went on to explain about light years and the immense vastness of space. I don't know how much I understood, but I did grasp that planet Earth was a tiny place compared to the universe. And if the earth itself was tiny, what did that say about me?

It was an awesome moment. I distinctly remember thinking, I'm not even as big as a mosquito, which was the smallest living creature I could think of. I'm sure I didn't know the word "awe," but that's the feeling that crept over me.

When we try to comprehend the immensity of our world, our galaxy, or even the universe, and realize that God brought all of it into existence with a mere "Let there be ...," it fills us with awe.

Yet the Bible assures us that, in the midst of all that vastness God sees each of us *individually*. What an awesome God. And that God loves me.

When we consider the writings of the church fathers and Reformers, we realize they understood the majestic God who created and ruled the universe—a concept we seem to have lost. They tiptoed into the presence of the awe-inspiring God; we charge in demanding answers and solutions. Reverence and deep, deep homage permeate their writings; we speak to the Holy One in the most familiar, mundane terms and consider reverence as a carry-over from a boring formalism.

We have difficulty even reading the definition of God in the Westminster Confession of Faith (1643–1647): "There is but one living and true God, who is infinite in being and perfection, a most pure spirit, invisible, without body, parts or passions, immutable, immense, eternal, incomprehensible, almighty, most wise, most holy, most free, most absolute, working in all things according to the counsel of His own immutable and most righteous will, for His own glory; most loving, gracious, forgiving iniquity, transgression, and sin; the rewarder of them that diligently seek Him; and withal most just and terrible in just judgments; hating all sin, and who will by no means clear the guilty" (Chapter II, 1).

Why don't we try to recapture the concept of the awesome God envisioned by those godly scholars three centuries ago? They perceived God with a holy reverence that seems lost in our world. They referred to God as the One with absolute knowledge who is "holy in all his counsels." They said that worship, service, and obedience are due to God. Those divines of old spoke of God's power and reminded us of who it is that commands the elements of nature to obey, who declares the hours of light and darkness, who makes the planets rotate in order, and who brings seedtime and harvest.

It is our awesome God.

Shortly after I began my new way of praying to various facets of God's personhood, I worshiped in a small church. In their informal style, the congregation sang a number of choruses. Two of them contained the line, "Our God is an awesome God." Many raised their hands and closed their eyes in what seemed like genuine worship. Across the aisle from me, an elderly woman stopped singing as tears slid down her cheeks. Yes, maybe they have discovered something of the awesomeness of God, I thought, as I sang.

Ours is the privilege to come into the presence—to invade the privacy—of an awesome God. Yet we moderns face a danger—danger of familiarity. We're no longer like our fourth-grade class at the planetarium when we felt an overpowering awe as we stared into the skies. Now we have space shuttles that fly to the moon or orbit the earth—scientific breakthroughs that tend to lessen our sense of awe. TV satellites, the Hubble telescope, and the discovery of a new planet in early 1996—these make everything feel closer, smaller and less significant. We can't quite reach the most distant star with today's technology, but we know it's only a matter of time until we do. As our awe over the universe increases, sadly, our awe of God declines.

We need to recapture that sense of wonder and majesty about God that is so lost to our world. How do we do that? One way is to consider all that the powerful Creator of the world has brought into being for us.

As I write this, spring has returned to the land with a lushness that seemed impossible in November. In my yard, red tulips bloom and squirrels race up and down the trees. As I look outside my window at the first hints of the flowering dogwoods, I begin to sing:

> *This is my Father's world:*
> *The birds their carols raise,*
> *The morning light, the lily white,*
> *Declare their Maker's praise.*
>
> *This is my Father's world:*
> *He shines in all that's fair;*
> *In the rustling grass, I hear Him pass,*
> *He speaks to me everywhere.*
>
> Maltbie D. Babcock, 1901.

Yes, our God is an awesome God who invites us into the divine presence.

⚜ ⚜ ⚜

Then God said, "Let the earth produce every sort of animal, each producing offspring of the same kind—livestock, small animals that scurry along the ground, and wild animals." And that is what happened (Genesis 1:24).

Awesome God,
how do I begin to comprehend your majestic power?
How do I take in the world you brought into being
and continue to sustain?
How do I grasp that you've created everything
from earthworms to water-laden skies
to bring harmony to this planet?
It's beyond my comprehension.
The best I can do is to stare at your created world,
remember that it's your footstool,
and whisper in hushed tones,
"Thank you, Awesome God,
for the vastness of this world,
and for your love for the human race
that prompted its creation." Amen.

Chapter Two
The Exclusive God

Wanda poked her head around the corner and giggled. "Cec. Your name is Cec," she said and giggled again. "That's what everyone calls you."

I picked up my five-year-old daughter and sat her on my knee. "That's right, honey," I said. "They *have* to call me that. But you don't. In fact, you can call me something none of them can call me. It's a name that only you and your sister C-C and baby John Mark can call me."

Her dark eyes widened. "Just us? Nobody else?"

"Nobody else. Nobody in the whole world. You can call me *Daddy*, and none of them can. Just you three and no one else. It's a special name only you can use."

Her face lit up. She dropped from my lap, and I heard her calling C-C. "We're the only ones who can call him Daddy!"

That's a bit like our relationship to the Exclusive God. We don't usually use the name Daddy, although that's all right. Both Jesus and the apostle Paul used

Abba—a term that denotes childlike intimacy and trust in God the Father.

When I refer to the Exclusive God, I don't mean that God doesn't love every individual in the world. However, the Bible states clearly that believers have an exclusive relationship with God, one reserved for those who belong to God's family.

We can also use a special name properly limited to God's people. It's what we call the covenant name; it is exclusively for those who are part of what many refer to as the covenant community. (Covenant is a theological term for agreement or testament, as in New Testament. God's most important covenants were the ones with Israel and the new covenant through Jesus Christ. Both covenants mean God made a contract to be the God of those who entered into agreement.)

Under the old covenant, God's revelation was through an exclusive name, and we don't even know how to pronounce it. The Hebrew Bible was written without vowels, and letters such as *J* and *Y*, as well as *V* and *W*, are interchangeable. The consonants in God's name are either *JHVH* (in times past, pronounced Jehovah) or *YHWH* (Yahweh, the more recent pronunciation). Regardless of how it's pronounced, it's a name reserved only for those who are part of God's covenant community.

Although we know the name, we don't know exactly what it means. The closest we can come is "I AM WHO I AM" or "I am the one who is, who was, and who ever shall be." It means that God is infinite and that no one can begin to define God except God. In most translations, they write the special name as LORD—a capital followed by small capital letters.

The use of the exclusive name began with Moses at the burning bush. He heard the words, "I am Yahweh—'the Lord.' I appeared to Abraham, to Isaac, and to Jacob as El-Shaddai—'God Almighty'—but I did not reveal my name, Yahweh, to them" (Exodus 6:2–3). When God spoke to Moses, a new relationship began. God revealed himself as the absolute Being who made and kept promises.

Although the covenant is open to everyone, it's like any other family or organization. There are conditions. In the Old Testament, as an act of faith in their relationship as the chosen people, Jews circumcised male infants on the eighth day. This was a son's rite of entry into the covenant family. In the New Testament, we cite water baptism as the outward rite of entry into the covenant community. Paul's letter to the Romans (chapters 9 through 11) argues that we who are non-Jews have been grafted into the tree of Israel because of Jesus Christ. That engrafting makes us members of the covenant community and eligible to use the sacred name. It's a privilege not to be taken lightly. When we pray to Yahweh, we pray to God as one with whom we have a unique relationship.

In some ways it's like belonging to an exclusive club—not that others can't join, because God extends the invitation to everyone. Instead of barring others from this exclusive relationship, God urges us to invite them into the special covenant. Once they have come to God, they too become members of that special family the apostle Paul calls the Israel of God (see Galatians 6:16).

When we speak to Yahweh, we remind *ourselves* that we're part of the people with whom God has entered into agreement. This relationship gives us permission—even a boldness—to talk to God.

For example, before I became a Christian, I sometimes prayed, "God, if you exist and if you're willing to listen to me ..." I didn't know if I was good enough to pray or if God would listen to me. Until I entered into the covenant community and understood the Exclusive God, I would have had no right to pray, "Our Father ...," "Loving Lord ...," "Compassionate God ...," or "Yahweh...." How could I? I hadn't yet joined the family of the covenant community. I hadn't yet experienced the embrace of the Exclusive God.

Being part of the covenant community speaks of mutuality. We've entered into an agreement. The often-quoted promise states the relationship well: "Then if my people who are called by my name will humble themselves and pray and seek my face and turn from their wicked ways, I will hear from heaven and will forgive their sins and restore their land" (2 Chronicles 7:14).

This Bible verse describes the two-way relationship of prayer. When we pray, we examine ourselves and confess any wrongdoings. Then—on the basis of God's covenant promises to us—we ask God to work on our behalf. Our relationship doesn't guarantee us what we want, but it does assure us that we have the right to pray and that God listens.

Praying to Yahweh reminds us of an intimate divine-human relationship. Yahweh is the one who knows all our troubles, who comforts us in our pain, and whispers to us in times of despair. Yahweh disciplines us and says, "I correct and discipline everyone I love" (see Revelation 3:19).

We belong to God. No matter how terrible our situations seem, this assures us we're in a special relationship with Yahweh, who is, who was, and who ever shall be.

> For the honor of your name, O LORD, forgive my many, many sins. Who are those who fear the LORD? He will show them the path they should choose. The LORD is a friend to those who fear him. He teaches them his covenant (Psalm 25:11–12, 14).

Exclusive God,
thanks for making me part of your covenant people,
for allowing me to be part of your exclusive community—
a people you love and care for always. Amen.

Chapter Three
The Eternal One

"But who made God?" I must have been not more than six years old when I asked my mother.

"Nobody made God," she said, "He always was and always will be."

"But before that?" I persisted. "I mean before all the things God did, who made God?"

She shook her head and gave me a long explanation, which didn't make any more sense to me than her first answer. After she walked away, I thought, she doesn't know either.

At age six, it seemed impossible for something not to have a beginning. "There had to be a place to start," I mumbled to myself, "even if it was a long, long, long time ago."

In college, one of my scientifically minded friends tried to explain it to me. He threw in a lot of scientific verbiage about the relativity of time, that it was circular and not linear, but I was as confused at age twenty as I had been at six.

Now, decades later, my theology and my Bible tell me God is, was, and always will be. I accept this as the final word.

I've never found a satisfactory solution to understanding the eternity of God and I assume I never will. My friend, Jay Zinn, said, "You know, we're created beings. Everything in our world is created from something else. I had a dad who had a dad who had a dad. I can't understand anything about humans or animals or plants except to look for what they came from. But God is above and beyond creation. And we can't understand something that's beyond the created world we live in."

I agreed with Jay, but it didn't stop me from asking and trying to understand. I still believe in trying to make sense of the mysteries of the universe. Yet I also realize how this works for me in daily, practical living. I want explanations. I want to understand. "God, make it clear" is something I've often prayed. The phrase "I just don't understand" is such a habitual part of my prayer life, it wouldn't seem natural to pray about difficulties without using it.

For instance, as a writer, I pray for God to help me write a book. I write it, and then I pray for God to help me sell it to a publisher. I get turned down. I try a second time and get another rejection. I pray, "God, I just don't understand. You want me to be happy, or fulfilled, or at peace, so why do I go through all this?"

I pray for my friend who is in danger of losing her job and she gets fired. Larry goes on a diet; I pray for God to help him lose forty pounds. After three weeks, he has lost nothing and abandons his weight-loss program. "I don't understand," is my answer.

In hundreds of ways I don't understand what God is doing in my life or in anyone else's. But one day I realized that was precisely the problem: I put the emphasis on understanding.

The day that light crept in, I had just read the words of Brother Lawrence, who contrasted our understanding with the act of our will. Understanding, he said, is of little benefit, but the commitment of our will is of immense value.

Then I got it. I would say it like this. I kept wanting to obey the Eternal One after I understood the divine plan. Instead, God wanted me to commit my will even if I didn't understand.

I found help in this matter recently when I came across a typed sheet of paper that someone gave me many years ago. I know only that it's called "Others May, You Cannot" by George Watson. Here is part of one paragraph:

... make up your mind that God is an infinite Sovereign and has a right to do as he pleases with his own. He may not explain to you a thousand things which puzzle your reason in his dealings with you, but if you absolutely sell yourself to be his love slave, he will wrap you up in a jealous love and bestow upon you many blessings....

God has no obligation to explain anything to me. It's the matter of the creature trying to usurp the role of Creator to demand such explanations or understandings. I'm willing to let the Eternal One work out all the solutions to the problems of this time and the period beyond human time.

I'm also learning to be grateful that God is here with us now, reminding us who *is* the Eternal One. I don't have to understand the Eternal One, I need only commit myself.

> For the LORD is God, and he created the heavens and earth and put everything in place. He made the world to be lived in, not to be a place of empty chaos. "I am the LORD," he says, "and there is no other. I, the LORD, speak only what is true and declare only what is right" (Isaiah 45:18–19).

Eternal and Everlasting God,
I don't understand such terms as eternal and everlasting.
How can I? My world is limited and temporal.
Whether I understand isn't the issue, is it?
Help me commit my will totally to you,
especially when I don't understand
what you're doing with my life
or the lives of others around me. Amen.

Chapter Four
The All-Seeing One

"Okay, God, what do I do now? How do I handle this situation?"

Most of us have asked these and similar questions countless times in prayer. Questions like these usually imply we're ready to do something as soon as the All-Seeing One directs. We want to take action.

Sometimes, however, we don't need to do anything; we simply need to see the situation differently. In recent days, the word *see* has become operative in my prayers to God for help.

For example, suppose I'm aware of a number of problems among my friends. Phil and his son are at odds; unless something happens, Marie and Jim will end up in divorce court; a man I care about very much has started to drink and I suspect it's taking over his life. As I have become aware of these and other situations, my natural inclination is to do something. I want to fix things.

Yet the Bible shows me that Jesus didn't rush to the rescue. When he heard that his friend Lazarus was sick, he didn't set off for Bethany. He waited until it was God's time for him to go (see John 11). He refused to act despite the voices around him that cried, "Do something."

When we pray, "Show me what to do," it implies that we believe God wants us to do something. Instead, God may want us to hear the words, "Be quiet. Do nothing."

I don't find it easy to hear the voice that stops me from jumping into action, but I've developed a way to approach God in perplexing situations. I offer my prayer to the All-Seeing One who knows the end from the beginning. I say, "Let me see this situation from the right perspective." When I—or any of us—pray these words, we are opening ourselves to hear God's marching orders—or stopping orders.

It isn't always easy, but we can learn to ask God to allow us to see the situation and show us where or how we fit into the solution—that is, if we do fit in at all. Maybe the All-Seeing One doesn't want us actively involved. As we ask God to open that all-seeing vision to us, we may become aware that we're to do nothing. When this happens, we can pray for those involved to come up with a solution.

For instance, how many times do we see things that we're convinced need to be changed at church? Some of us, with our limited view of the entire church program, could come up with a list of twenty things to make a healthier, happier church. Maybe our ideas are good—even brilliant—but our involvement may not be the mandate of the All-Seeing One.

Praying to the All-Seeing God can be extremely liberating. We realize that we don't have to put out every fire or be the rescuer in every situation. It reminds us that God-Who-Sees-All will direct us: when to take action, when to remove our hands, and when to pray for others to intervene.

I recall how this worked for me in one situation with a business associate. A problem had risen that did not involve me directly. However, I was sure I knew the solution, and decided to write him a letter. Ordinarily, I would have prayed, "God, show me what to write. Direct my words." But I wanted to straighten out the other person involved; I believed that unless I did something, the situation wouldn't work out. Everything hinged on my actions.

I started to write the letter but then stopped. I was taking action before I heard God speak. I stopped, turned away from my computer, and prayed. "All-Seeing One, help me see what to do in this situation. Where do I fit into it?"

I waited for God to give me some glorious ideas to zap out on my computer. I heard nothing. No words came. I continued to wait. Within a few minutes, I *knew* the answer: It wasn't my problem to resolve. The other person hadn't asked me to solve it anyway.

Such incidents help me realize I don't have everything in life figured out. I've grasped enough, though, to realize that I am limited by my own senses, except when God graciously imparts insight. Like many others, I tend to see myself in the center of the vast universe and, in that position, I have to respond to everything that affects me. But sometimes, God doesn't call us to respond. Sometimes a loving God allows us only to see. And when we see, maybe it's God's call for us to pray to the All-Seeing One to act.

> I will instruct you and teach you in the way you should go; I will guide you with My eye (Psalm 32:8, NKJV).
>
> The LORD says, "I will guide you along the best pathway for your life. I will advise you and watch over you" (Psalm 32:8).

All-Seeing God,
forgive me
for rushing into action;
forgive me for being so presumptuous to think
I must always be poised to act;
forgive me for not allowing you to show me
what I need to know in a situation.
Teach me always to ask you to let me see
what I need to see. Amen.

Chapter Five
The Wholly Other

During my first year of seminary, the professors and other students talked about God as "Wholly Other." Sometimes they used terms such as the "Transcendent God" and the "Self-Existent One." The idea our professors tried to get through to us is that God was totally different from human creation.

It hit me powerfully to think of the impassable gulf between God and us. One of the major points of our theological discussions was that we ourselves could never bridge the gap. God had to break through and reach toward us.

The concept meant a great deal to me. It implied that before we ever get around to thinking about reaching upward, God already has reached downward and clasped our hands.

This doctrine of the Wholly Other reminds me of my limited view of life, my extremely finite wisdom and perception. Isaiah put it this way: "My thoughts are nothing like your thoughts," says the LORD. "And my ways are far beyond anything you could imagine. For just as the heavens are higher than the earth, so my ways are higher than your ways and my thoughts higher than your thoughts" (Isaiah 55:8–9). God is completely different from us—the Wholly Other.

I catch a glimpse of this when I remember an incident from my childhood. I couldn't have been more than nine years old. We lived in the west end of Davenport, Iowa. One day I went walking alone and got lost in the east end of town. From the road where I was walking, I saw huge homes on large tracts of land, all of them high above the street and facing the Mississippi River. I stared at the immense houses and wondered what kind of people lived there.

On a whim I decided to race across the street and get a view of the houses from the river side. I darted out and didn't see a car coming out of a nearby driveway. The driver didn't see me either until it was too late. He knocked me down.

I wasn't hurt, but I was scared. I don't remember much about the people that were there, except for a woman who wore a fur coat and a necklace made of what I assumed were real diamonds. (Except for in movies, I'd never seen any.)

The driver stopped and tried to help me. I got up to walk away. He insisted on taking me to his doctor, but I kept saying no, that I was fine. He finally demanded that I get inside his car, which I did. He drove me back up to his house and we went inside while he phoned the doctor.

Ten minutes later, I was in a doctor's office in the business section of town. I was fine. When I left, I knew my location and went back home on foot.

While I was in the man's house, I had felt out of place. Although he was kind to me, I knew I didn't belong there. This is even more true when I am in God's awesome presence—I feel I don't belong there. I'm a sinful human being, a man who makes a lot of mistakes every day. Isaiah had it right—God's thoughts are too high for me.

When I contemplate the Wholly Other-ness of God, I keep wondering why God would come to us. I've heard sermons about God wanting human companionship, and maybe that's the answer. But I feel sure it wasn't because God was lonely or needed us. In fact, that's what makes this so marvelous to me. I can't think of one reason God would reach down to the human race. We deserve nothing, and God owes us nothing. We fail God at every point of decision. Still, the Wholly Other's hand reaches downward, and we hear, "I have loved you, my people, with an everlasting love. With unfailing love I have drawn you to myself" (Jeremiah 31:3).

There is a passage in Deuteronomy where God speaks through Moses to the Jewish nation before they went into the land. He talks to them about their relationship: "For you are a holy people, who belong to the LORD your God. Of all the people on earth, the LORD your God has chosen you to be his own special treasure. The LORD did not set his heart on you and choose you because you were more numerous than other nations, for you were the smallest of all nations! Rather, it was simply that the LORD loves you, and he was keeping the oath he had sworn to your ancestors" (Deuteronomy 7:6–8).

God affirms a special relationship with Israel, calls them a holy people, and says this is only "because the LORD loves you." There is no other reason given there or elsewhere. God simply chooses to love humanity. That's the closest we can get to solving the divine mystery.

God is Wholly Other, and my mind can't grasp it. But I can believe it.

And it is to the Wholly Other that I can pray.

> The high and lofty one who lives in eternity, the Holy One, says this: "I live in the high and holy place with those whose spirits are contrite and humble. I restore the crushed spirit of the humble and revive the courage of those with repentant hearts" (Isaiah 57:15).

Wholly Other God,
as soon as I begin to sense
that I've figured you out,
you show me how little I really know about you.
Thank you, God, that there is always more of you
than I can understand,
and thanks also for enabling me to understand
as much as I do. Amen.

Chapter Six
The Immanent, Present One

"I went to that church for twenty years," he said, "and I never once heard the gospel."

"That's probably right," I said. "The pastor preached, but you just didn't hear it." My friend didn't like my response, but I had known the man who pastured that church during the years he was referring to. A solid evangelical, that pastor wouldn't have preached without showing the people the way to God.

Yet, in hindsight, my friend's complaint makes sense to me, because there was a time when I didn't hear the gospel either. In my pre-conversion days, when I thought of God, I entertained vague concepts of the All-Powerful, All-Seeing, All-Knowing One. During my few visits to Sunday school as a child, I heard about the Holy God who wouldn't look upon sin. I recall a lot of lessons about divine judgment at the end of the world. But I didn't learn much about

God, the Immanent One. I heard the gospel many times, but I never "got it" until I was ready to accept God's love.

When the theologians use that heady term *immanent* they simply mean that God is present everyplace, or God is with us. For me, this is one of the best ways to think about God and a relationship with him. Maybe because it brings this message to my consciousness again and again, Psalm 139 is my favorite. It begins: "O Lord, you have examined my heart and know everything about me. You know when I sit down or stand up. You know my thoughts even when I'm far away. You see me when I travel and when I rest at home. You know everything I do" (vv. 1–3). This aspect of God's personality appeals to me. God is here, involved, and directing traffic in every area of my life.

I'm not one of those who sees God in rocks or drops of water. Those people usually tell me that I don't really need to pray because god is in me, and I am god, so if I pray, I am only praying to myself.

I do, however, love the idea that God not only created all things in this world, but did it for our enjoyment. I believe that God and I can enjoy it together. For instance, when I work at my computer, I frequently glance out my window. The yard slopes downhill and there's a creek below. A large oak grows near the house, and I sometimes pause to watch the squirrels play games, racing up and down its trunk. When I see those sights, it often makes me think of God's glorious creation. It gladdens me that

I have a personal relationship with the Artist and Creator of the world, and I pause to say, "Thanks." In my mental imaging, God smiles at the results of a glorious creation.

I relish the concept of the immanence of God. It gives me a sense of the closeness, the care, and the protective hand of God in my life. That leads me once again to Psalm 139. The writer tries to examine every aspect of his life, and in so doing, realizes God is part of all of it. Before he speaks, God knows what he's going to say (v. 4); God protects him (v. 5); no matter where he goes, he's never out of God's sight (vv. 7–12).

These thoughts lead me to appreciate God as the Immanent One—the Present One—who is my companion wherever I go. I concentrate on the God, as the old hymn goes, *"who walks with me and talks with me and tells me I am His own."*

As I try to envision the implications of God's immanence, I get a mental picture from the story of the Garden of Eden. We read that, after Adam and Eve had eaten the forbidden fruit and realized they were naked:

"When the cool evening breezes were blowing, the man and his wife heard the Lord God walking about in the garden. So they hid from the Lord God among the trees" (Genesis 3:8).

I can't visualize God, of course, but the words convey a powerful image to me. That couple actually walked with God in the cool of the day. What would it be like, literally, to walk in the garden with God?

What kind of presence was there for them to see or touch?

To say "God is here and everywhere" doesn't mean much, so I like to personalize the immanence of God. When we lie down at night and drift off to sleep, why not think of God as standing next to our beds, tucking us in by the divine presence? We can speak good night words, or when we open our eyes in the morning, God's face is smiling at us, and we can give thanks for the sleep. It gives me great pleasure to think of God being part of everything that happens in my life and being beside me wherever I go.

God is here, right now. Everyplace we are can be a holy place because of God's presence. When I first realized this years ago, it changed my whole concept of prayer. Until then, I had the idea that I had to pray on bended knees and with closed eyes. That's one way to pray. But when I contemplate the Immanent God, I can pray anytime and anywhere.

You are with me, God.

That knowledge brings me peace and joy.

> O Lord, you have examined my heart and know everything about me (Psalm 139:1).
>
> [Jesus said,] "... I am with you always, even to the end of the age" (Matthew 28:20).

Cecil Murphey

⚜ ⚜ ⚜

Immanent One,
you're here, right now, and in this place.
Always. Thank you. Amen.

Chapter Seven
The God of the Sacrament

At Emmanuel Baptist Church—the first church I ever joined—they concluded the fourth Sunday worship with Communion. I didn't like those Sundays very much. Following Pastor Olsen's thirty-minute-plus sermon, deacons served us bread and juice. We didn't get out of church on those Sundays until nearly 12:30.

Every time, our pastor reminded us that it was a memorial service. He quoted Paul's words, that we were observing "the Lord's death till he come."

In the Communion service at another church, elders served the bread and we held it in our hand until everyone was served. The waiting caused my palms to sweat as I focused on my fear of dropping the bread. When the juice was served, I concentrated mainly on holding the half-ounce juice glass without tipping it over while I waited for the other three-hundred-plus members to be served. During those waiting periods, I concentrated more on sitting still and not dropping or spilling than I did with what was supposed to be happening with the bread and juice.

Although my theological training has since taught me otherwise, for a long time I saw little special about chewing a morsel of dry, tasteless bread and washing it down with a thimbleful of grape juice. I had read all the theological positions regarding the sacrament and I could explain the different views held by Catholics, Lutherans, Presbyterians, and Baptists. But, in practice, the Communion service held little real meaning for me. I considered it more of an academic or theological exercise.

It is likely I would have remained that way, except I began to read some classic writings of the past. When I encountered the small classic, *The Practice of the Presence of God,* I noticed that Brother Lawrence, its author, made several references to the "blessed sacrament." I read Luther and Calvin and the Puritan Reformers of England. Their writings began to influence my thinking immensely, and the importance they placed on the sacrament amazed me.

If those leading voices wrote so heatedly about it, I reasoned, I needed to reexamine what it means when we celebrate the Lord's Supper. What does God want me to grasp from this? I asked myself.

Eventually, after much study of different views, I came to believe in the *spiritual presence* of Jesus Christ. I don't personally think other viewpoints are wrong—those who formulated the various positions were much brighter than I am—but I opted for what has provided the most satisfaction for me intellectually and emotionally.

Now when I go forward and stand around a table to receive bread and grape juice (as we do in our particular congregation), I pause to remind myself that Jesus Christ is present with me all the time, but especially in those moments when I symbolically eat his body and drink his blood. Now when I receive the sacrament, I silently thank Jesus Christ for strengthening me and drawing me closer.

Although it took years for me to grasp, now when I hold the bread or the cup, I have an awareness that God is present in a special, unexplainable way. Emotionally, I don't always feel awe or praise; sometimes, I take it quite mechanically. And yet even then, I say to myself, "Jesus Christ, your grace is being infused into me." I like the idea of believing that when I approach Jesus Christ through the sacrament, it's one more way for me to move toward a fuller commitment to God.

At times I envision Jesus in the Upper Room with his twelve disciples. He offers them what theologians call the "elements" of bread and wine. Even though others stand on both sides of me, I like to think of his saying just to me, "Cec, this is my body—my life—that I'm laying down out of love for you." Then, "Cec, this symbol of my blood is to let you know that I chose to die for you."

That's when I catch glimpses of the meaning of the passion story: The Innocent One dying for me, a sinner; the Holy One making the unclean one clean; the Giver of Life extending eternal life to the death-certified human.

In the quietness of the passing of the elements, I am aware of Jesus Christ being present with me. He is in front of me, beside me, behind me, around me, and for a few moments I have a profound sense of being in a holy place.

I'm reminded that I've been forgiven. Because God has wiped away all the past failures, I'm starting all over again. In those seconds of time, I often feel a sense of deep inner renewal.

As I participate in the sacrament, I'm also aware that I'm not alone. Not only are there other people in the building with me, but there are people around the world who are with me. Paul, Peter, Timothy, Lydia, and all the saints of old have shared these same moments of imparted grace.

I often think of the first time I knelt in an Episcopal church. We cupped our hands to receive the bread. The rector explained that we were coming as supplicants, asking for the bread of life. An assistant handed us a wafer and then tipped the cup to our lips. "Think of yourself as dying, and I bring to you the blood of Jesus Christ as a transfusion," he said. "It saves your life and restores you to health. That is the purpose of this sacrament."

As I knelt, my hands cupped, I truly felt like a supplicant, seeking the favor of God, waiting for the wafer to be placed in my palm. As I received it and in the seconds before I ate it, I thought, Yes, God, this is a holy moment. You are here with me. You are here because you love me.

"You are my Sacrament, Lord Jesus," I prayed silently. "This is our moment of true communion."

For us, Communion can be exactly what the word implies: joint union with God. We pray to the One who reminds us of the greatest gift of all—the death of the innocent Son for us, the guilty.

> Now, most people would not be willing to die for an upright person, though someone might perhaps be willing to die for a person who is especially good. But God showed his great love for us by sending Christ to die for us while we were still sinners (Romans 5:7–8).

God of the Sacrament,
you offer me your loving presence.
You accept me always.
Most of all, you showed me the extent of your love
through the death of Jesus Christ.
Help me grasp the extent of that loving gift to me. Amen.

Chapter Eight
The True Father

"We don't use that word around here," started the Christian educator as she glared at me. "*Father* is not part of our vocabulary." When I challenged her reasoning, she said, "Many of these children come from terrible homes. They have no idea what a good father is like. The only father they know is one who beat them or sold their toys for drugs or alcohol."

"Maybe that's all the more reason to talk to them about God the Father," I said. I might as well have saved my breath; she wouldn't consider that I might have a valid point. Yet I knew she understood the trauma of many of her students.

"Let me tell you something," I said before I left. "I had no idea of what a good father was either. But the concept of God as a Father helped bring me into the faith." She raised an eyebrow at that remark, but said nothing more.

I understood her reasoning, but I didn't agree with it. When I was in my early twenties, I heard the first sermon I can remember about the fatherhood of God. I sat in the stark building, on a pew without a cushion, and wondered why I had bothered to attend anyway. I had come alone on a whim; going to church wasn't part of my regular Sunday activities. The liturgy confused me, the music bored me, and I never seemed to know where we were reading in the Bible. I didn't care about a lengthy report from the vestry or a summary of the triennial conference.

Finally, the robed minister stood to preach. "Do you want to understand God?" He went on to say that if we want to grasp who God is, the best way is to think of God as a loving, caring father. I particularly recall one sentence: "Because he embodies all qualities of earthly fathers in their highest form, we refer to him as our heavenly Father."

For the first time in my life, I understood that God was *like a father who loves and wants only the best for his kids*. Every action God does on our behalf is an act of love. It made me realize that God could fill that deep void in my life that my own father had never satisfied.

The rector said our human, earthly fathers failed us in many ways, and that's why we need to see God as the perfect parent—the one who would never fail us, the one who treats each of us as special children.

I could track with that. My dad was an alcoholic. When he was sober, he was kind and had a delightful sense of humor. With a few beers inside him, he became harsh and short-tempered. I received a number of undeserved beatings, a lot of blaming for things I didn't do, and a feeling that no matter what I did, it wouldn't be good enough.

Yes, I knew about an earthly father, and it wasn't much to inspire me. Then I heard about a heavenly Father who is different. He's the Father who wraps loving arms around us, who listens to us, and most of all, who understands our pain.

In the years since then, I've learned a lot of theology, but I suspect I never grasped anything more profound than I did that day in church. It would still be months before I fully turned to God, but that was one of the early seeds of understanding.

God is like a Father who never fails us. Today I would say that the father-need in us is part of our brain's hardwiring; we have no real inner peace until we find fulfillment for that need. I found that fulfillment in God the True Father.

Even today, when I pray to God the Father, sometimes I have a mental image of myself as a preschooler. I sit on his lap. I babble away about the things that trouble me. I feel his strong arms surrounding me and his warm embrace as he whispers, "I have loved you with an everlasting love."

Sometimes I think about my own son—the time when he stubbed his toe, the first time he fell off his bike, or the time he ran his first race and came in last. I was there. I held him and wiped away his tears. Yes, I know the tenderness of a father.

The more I envision God the Father, the more I see the God who invites intimacy and closeness. Granted, the relationship between fathers and children may have been different in biblical days, but I doubt it.

I lived in East Africa where I saw a lifestyle in rural areas that echoed the life of biblical days. It touched me to see how children behaved and related to their parents. A few times, parents yelled at young children, especially warning to stay away from the open fires or to watch their feet on the path to the river. But I never saw beatings, harsh treatment, or neglect.

More than once I have been sitting in a business meeting when a small child would walk inside, climb up into his father's lap, and lay his head on his shoulder. Without a word between them, the father held the child. It caused no disruption. That is a visual image of the fatherhood of God.

The Bible, of course, speaks about God the Father chastening his children, and I wouldn't want to ignore that concept. But most of us probably need to think more about the one who both Jesus and Paul addressed as Abba Father or Daddy God.

We can pray to our True Father who loves us, cares about every need in our lives, and provides a place of safety. That's the True Father.

> The Lord is like a father to his children, tender and compassionate to those who fear him (Psalm 103:13).

[Jesus said,] "Pray like this: Our Father in heaven, may your name be kept holy" (Matthew 6:9).

Abba Father,
as I approach you,
help me know that your hand holds mine,
that you're always there for me to lean on
because you hold me—
especially when I'm afraid,
alone, or troubled. Amen.

Chapter Nine
The Divine Connector

Alone? Misunderstood? Feel the need to belong? Those were the opening words of an ad our church once ran in the newspaper. Several people responded to it, and said, "That's me."

Of course, the truth is, it's everyone.

To be human is to feel estranged from others. It's to know and to live with loneliness. Some people won't allow themselves to feel it, or they're too numb, but I believe God created the hardwiring in our systems to make us yearn for belonging and togetherness with others. To sense the gulf between us is what the theologians call original sin—the act that separated humanity from unbroken fellowship with the Creator.

The truth is, one of the great longings all of us have is to belong. Some satisfy the longing by becoming groupies or members of an organization, such as the Church. Others never find a place to belong, but always remain on the outside peering in.

The Church, when we're at our best, comes about as close to meeting this human need as anything I've ever experienced. We share a commonality and we talk about our need for connectedness. Even though we don't always live up to that ideal, that's how God designed the Church to operate.

Our connection is not to a building or a denomination. We all have preferences; we like different architecture and divergent styles of worship. But God's design is to make us aware of the *potential* for connectedness with other humans, and to make us aware of the divine link that connects us. God makes us part of a special family—the family of God.

Perhaps I can explain it best by an experience I had in 1970. One of my seminary professors came to our church to preach and to celebrate the Lord's Supper with us. His words that morning opened a new world for me.

As Dr. Will Ormand stood in front of the table and gave the invitation, he said, "This is not a Presbyterian table. It's the Lord's Table, and the invitation is for all believers."

I had heard that before, of course. He went on to say, "It's the same table around which Jesus sat with his disciples in the Upper Room on the night of his betrayal. This is a table that connects each believer through the centuries to all believers everywhere."

His words transformed what had been just an intellectual concept inside my head into a deep sense of experienced knowledge. It wasn't a message that said, "Cec, you belong"; it was even more powerful. It said I was part of a long heritage, that I had been joined to the people of God who had been living and worshiping from the beginning of the human race.

Today, as I think of my spiritual heritage, I hear the words of God spoken to Moses. God heard their groaning, and he remembered his covenant promise to Abraham, Isaac, and Jacob (Exodus 2:24). "I am the God of your father—the God of Abraham, the God of Isaac, and the God of Jacob...." (Exodus 3:6). God also said to Moses, "Say this to the people of Israel: Yahweh, the God of your ancestors—the God of Abraham, the God of Isaac, and the God of Jacob—has sent me to you. This is my eternal name, my name to remember for all generations. Now go and call together all the elders of Israel. Tell them, 'The LORD, the God of your ancestors—the God of Abraham, Isaac, and Jacob—has appeared to me. He told me, "I have been watching closely, and I see how the Egyptians are treating you'" (Exodus 15–16).

Those aren't merely academic words or pronouncements that mean, "I'm the God of the Jews." The message is much, much more than that.

I saw this clearly in Mark's Gospel. The Sadducees (a liberal, religious group that didn't believe in miracles or the resurrection) tried to test Jesus. Under Jewish law if a married man died childless, the man's brother was to marry the widow.

They concocted an unlikely situation in which seven brothers died childless, each brother in turn having married the widow before she herself died. Their trick question was, "So tell us, whose wife will she be in the resurrection? For all seven were married to her" (Mark 12:23).

Jesus replied, "Your mistake is that you don't know the Scriptures, and you don't know the power of God. ... Haven't you ever read about this in the writings of Moses, in the story of the burning bush? Long after Abraham, Isaac, and Jacob had died, God said to Moses, 'I am the God of Abraham, the God of Isaac, and the God of Jacob.' So he is the God of the living, not the dead" (Mark 12:24, 2627).

Jesus spoke of an unbroken relationship that began with Abraham and continues onward through time and generations. God had entered into a relationship with Abraham, started a new nation with him, and carried on the covenant with each successive generation. The New Testament makes it clear that we are part of that spiritual lineage. The apostle Paul calls us—the Church—spiritual Israel (see Galatians 6:16). May God's peace and mercy be upon all who live by this principle; they are the new people of God.

To the Sadducees—and to us today—Jesus says that the eternal relationship with God is just that—eternal. God had been the friend of Abraham when he lived, and of Isaac, and of Jacob. That friendship didn't end with human death. God remains the God of those who have served God. We can also put our names right in God's words: "I am the God of

Abraham, and of Isaac, and of Jacob, and of Cec, and of Shirley, and of Scott...."

Our relationship with God places us in a line of spiritual heritage and into an ongoing, never-ending covenant with God. It is never broken—it can't be—whether we're alive on earth or in the heavenly presence of God. It's the divine connection because we belong to the Divine Connector.

The Lord's Table illustrates this clearly for me. When I take the bread and the juice, I'm confined to a single location, but the fellowship of which I'm a part extends throughout the whole world, and through all the generations of men and women, past, present, and even future.

I love the practice of many historic denominations that observe worldwide Communion Sunday on the first Sunday in October. It's a way of holding spiritual hands with sisters and brothers across the globe.

And it's more. It's the Divine Connector, linking us to others, all the way back to Abraham, Isaac, and Jacob.

This morning, just before sunrise, I walked through the wooded area near my house and prayed. I was alone, and I felt alone. I was wrestling with a couple of problems that involved other people, and it didn't seem as if a solution satisfactory to all of us would come about.

As I walked, the crunch of my shoes on the nature trail, the view of the river beeches, or the far-off cry of ducks at the lake didn't stir me as they usually do. I walked on, engulfed in my sense of estrangement from those others and a kind of malaise in general.

I thought of the Old Testament saints. Mentally, I saw Abraham picking up his entire family and moving from Ur of the Chaldees into a then-unknown area now known as Israel. I could see Jacob running in fear of his brother, Esau, and staying in exile for twenty years. I thought of Isaac when he walked through the fields alone at dusk.

Those men had known something of what I was feeling. They felt their separation from other humans. In those times, they had only one place to turn. They called out to God, the Divine Connector.

We share a commonality with each other through the centuries, and God is our connecting link. We can pray to the Great Connector who declares that we're in the line of the great succession of saints. As we open ourselves to God in prayer, we're walking alongside the innumerable multitude, linked to God, which also links us to others.

No, I'm not alone—not even alone with God. I am vitally connected to God's people no matter where I am or what my circumstances.

God heard their groaning, and he remembered his covenant promise to Abraham, Isaac, and Jacob. He looked down on the people of Israel and knew it was time to act (Exodus 2:24–25).

God of Abraham, Isaac, and Jacob,
thank you for connecting me to yourself.
Thank you for connecting me to all the saints who have
gone on before me,
and thank you for connecting me to
brothers and sisters now alive.
We are truly one in the Spirit, one in the Lord,
and for this, I'm immensely thankful. Amen.

Chapter Ten
Jacob's Father

In 1985, I finally faced the "Mel Syndrome."

Mel was my brother. In our family of seven children he was clearly the favorite of both our parents. I write *clearly* because the rest of us knew and acknowledged it—that is, everyone except my parents.

After I became a Christian, I discovered the joy of being a child of God and relished the concept of the Father's love I had never known.

Then, when I was spiritually ready, I confronted the "Mel Syndrome." When the trauma hit, I hurt so deeply that the pit of despair seemed to have no bottom. I was a man with grown kids, an empty nest, and a supportive wife. But I began to feel the pain of those long-buried memories from childhood.

For instance, when Mel (two years my junior) and I were in elementary school, Dad became ill. The illness kept him bedridden for weeks and jobless for months. After he got well, he started a job at a factory where they made aluminum nails and fences.

One Saturday, a few weeks after Dad had returned to work, he took Mel and me to Sears. He bought what he needed; we headed back toward his old Ford. In those days, the Sears stores placed a big candy counter in the center of the main floor. As we approached it, Mel said, "Hey, Dad, give me a dime."

My father fished into his overalls pocket, found a dime, and handed it to my brother. It wouldn't have occurred to me to ask Dad for a cent, because I knew he didn't have much money. Yet Mel's asking emboldened me.

"Could I have a nickel?" I asked.

"I don't have any more money," Dad said and walked on.

Mel had ten cents worth of marshmallow circus peanuts; I had nothing, even though my brother shared his candy with me.

If Mel asked, Mel received. If I asked, I didn't get what I wanted. Granted, my memories may be more vivid and painful than reality, but it is still the feeling I grew up with.

The years passed. My parents both died in the late 1970s and Mel died of the effects of alcoholism in 1983. In the last year of Mel's life, he and I talked often on the phone, even though he lived nearly a thousand miles away. We developed a friendship that only two long-estranged siblings could experience.

It was two years after his death that I experienced the "Mel Syndrome." The major symptom of the disease showed up when I prayed: It became increasingly difficult for me to ask God for anything. Even when I did ask, I didn't expect to receive, because I "knew" God wouldn't give me what I wanted. Pleading only made God more resistant in my mind.

The crisis erupted one day when I was doing my daily Bible reading. I had already read the Old Testament story of Esau and Jacob. My New Testament reading was Romans nine where, again, I read about the brothers. Although twins, Esau was born first. By tradition, he inherited a double portion of his father's wealth. But Jacob tricked his brother out of the inheritance and his father's blessing.

Did Jacob get punished? Was he cast into a pit of damnation? No, he became the head of the nation of Israel and a forefather of King David. I'd always thought of that as an act of grace on God's part.

When I read a portion of Romans 9, the "Mel Syndrome" hit in all its fury:

Yet before the twins were born or had done anything good or bad—in order that God's purpose in election might stand: not by works but by him who calls—she was told, "The older will serve the younger." Just as it is written: "Jacob I have loved, but Esau I hated." What then shall we say? Is God unjust? Not at all! For he says to Moses, "I will have mercy on whom I have mercy, and I will have compassion on whom I have compassion." It does not, therefore, depend on man's desire or effort, but on God's mercy (Romans 9:11–16, NIV).

As I read those verses a second time, the inner pain struck. *I was Esau.* God hated Esau. I had been

Esau in our family of origin. Mel was Jacob in our family. Without doing anything good or having to earn love, he was Dad's favorite—just like Jacob was favored by God.

Despite my efforts to stop them, the tears flowed. Years of pain surfaced. I realized how hard I had worked to win Dad's love, yet Mel had it without any effort; in fact, he treated my parents badly. I don't know how many times he borrowed money from them and never once paid back a cent. Yet Dad kept on lending to him.

By contrast, throughout my life, I had expended so much energy trying to please my father, trying to make him proud of me, trying to get the kind of acceptance and affirmation Mel had without doing anything.

Dad's affirmation and acceptance never came. And that day, when I made an emotional connection between Dad Murphey and Abba God, the hurt went beyond words. I was Esau, unwanted and unloved. Just as Dad had made his choice of Mel over me, God had done the same in rejecting Esau in favor of Jacob. It made no difference how Esau felt or what he might have done: The sovereign choice was made.

I knew on a *theological* level that I was fully acceptable to God, and that I was as loved by God as anyone else in the universe. John 3:16 and dozens of other verses make that fact unquestionable. But as my pain intensified, on an *emotional* level I *felt* as if God "so loved the *world*" (which included Cec Murphey) that he sent Jesus. That meant, God was stuck with me. I lucked into the total package and couldn't be turned down. After all, the Bible says anyone who comes to God won't be turned away.

During those dark days, I constantly cried out to Abba Father as Esau had once called to his father Isaac, "Is there no blessing left for me?" I didn't mind that Mel or Jacob received favor—and in my heart I believed they deserved it somehow. But I wanted to know that I was loved as a father's child.

But still the hurt feelings persisted. Yes, God was my heavenly Father. But after all, I was only Esau and not Jacob. To make it worse, there was no way I would ever be anything but Esau.

One day when I was alone in the woods, I screamed out in anger at God. "I've tried so hard to be good. I've tried to be the kind of Christian you want me to be and look at the way you treat me!"

That was my first breakthrough. I had tried to earn Abba Father's love just as I had tried to earn it from Dad. I never (to my way of feeling) got it from Dad. I always had it from Abba, but I didn't know it.

In a way that I can't now put into words, I had to separate the two fathers. I had to draw a line between an imperfect relationship and a perfect one. And it took a long, long time. But gradually, I began to distinguish Abba God from Dad. My dad, regardless of his motives, was imperfect at love, imperfect at parenting, and imperfect in every area of his life. God is not imperfect.

Ever so slowly, the concept sank deep into my heart that God used the term *Father* precisely to show us the perfect image of fatherhood. It took me years (I'm a slow learner) to accept that the Perfect Father could love imperfect children.

One morning, I heard myself say, "Wait a minute, I'm not Esau. I'm Jacob!" It was just that simple. Then I knew the Mel Syndrome no longer had any power over me. When that insight came to me, I could say, understand, and mean the words, "I am loved."

All of us who are believers are spiritual Jacobs. We can pray to the Forgiving Father, the Loving Parent who never turns us away. God said to Jacob: "What's more, I am with you, and I will protect you wherever you go. One day I will bring you back to this land. I will not leave you until I have finished giving you everything I have promised you" (Genesis 28:15).

That promise is ours as we pray to our Father.

> Even if my father and mother abandon me, the LORD will hold me close (Psalm 27:10).

> *Abba Father, Jacob's Father,*
> *I am Jacob and I am loved.*
> *You are my Father and you love me with*
> *the Perfect Father love.*

Chapter Eleven
My Owner

"I own you!"

"*Nobody* owns me."

If we watch TV, we've heard that dialogue many times, and we applaud the person who refuses to be intimidated. The response is a way of saying, "I'm my own boss. I'm in control of my life."

That's good, typical Western thinking. We like the idea of being in charge of our own lives. "This is my life," we say, "and I'm living it *my way.*"

That attitude contrasts sharply with the biblical teaching. In the New Testament, the writers tell us that we surrender to God or we serve the devil. We "sell our souls" either to God or to our selfish desires.

In older times, writers used the metaphor of selling our souls to the devil. Charles Gounod's 1859 opera, *Faust*, relates the tale of a man who sells his soul to the devil in return for knowledge and supernatural abilities.

Many modern films and books are based on this premise. Someone yearns for something badly and says, "I'd give my soul for that." Then along comes the evil character, disguised as good, who says, "I'll grant your desires in return for your soul." The person, deluded by desire, consents. And we know the rest of the story. The person gets everything he or she has ever desired. Eventually, though, the central character awakens to the stupidity of the agreement, and says, "Hey, wait a minute. It's a poor bargain. I'm not selling my soul."

These stories nearly always give us happy endings, because the characters figure out some trick to outsmart the devil and win back their souls.

We don't want to identify with those who have sold their souls. We like to think, "I am the master of my fate, I am the captain of my soul" (from "Invictus" by William Ernest Henley). It suits us better to think that we—and we alone—decide our fate.

Frankly, there's something good about that attitude, because it speaks of determination, self-reliance, and courage. It says we don't see ourselves as little puffs of cloud tossed across the sky by capricious winds. But most of the time we delude ourselves. Far too many of us sell out to some force, idea, philosophy, or need.

As we journey through life, somewhere along the winding path we confront the fork in the road—a time when we have to decide who controls our lives. My time came when my wife had pleurisy, my two young daughters were both sick with colds, and I was in college. That rainy May afternoon, I had to study for two final exams; the girls couldn't play outside, so they kept demanding my attention. I had other problems as well. Financially, we had been barely scraping by. On my desk lay several small bills and a large heating bill we couldn't pay. The car's gas tank was almost at the zero spot, and I had to drive to school.

I faced that dark moment and wondered if it was worth following Jesus Christ. At 2:30 that afternoon, when everyone quieted a few minutes, I knelt by the sofa and prayed. My head was splitting, anger at life in general surged through me, and I couldn't understand why all the pressures were hitting me.

"I'm fed up with God," I remember saying. "I'm fed up with barely surviving and not getting ahead." As I knelt there, I decided to quit college, get a job, turn my back on "this religious stuff" and go back to my old way of life (uh, well, a modified version of it). For maybe thirty-eight seconds, I felt a marvelous freedom. I was my own person, and I could do whatever I wanted with my life.

Then I knew that wasn't true. A picture flashed into my mind. Once I had seen an ad for a rescue mission that aimed at curing alcoholics. The picture showed a man inside a whiskey bottle, his right hand stretched out as he reached for help.

"That's the way I am," I said. "I'm caught by God and I can't get out."

Then came a second image. It was a film about a planeload of people over the Pacific Ocean. They were having engine trouble, but the pilot said,

"We've passed the point of no return." He meant that it was closer to go on than to turn back.

"That's it exactly!" Anger seethed inside me. "I want to turn back, God, and you won't let me!" I couldn't scream aloud because of my family, but inside my head I shook my fist at God.

Finally exhausted, I stopped. God wouldn't let me go. It was closer for me to go forward to the end than to turn back. I had long passed the fork in the road when I could make a choice.

God owned me. I couldn't get away from God then or ever.

Slowly, a deep peace came over me. Within minutes, I felt all right, and even my headache lessened. I didn't know what I'd do about the tests the next day, but I had a family that came first.

I did study for a while. My daughters napped and when they awakened, they were quiet. The older one sat on my lap and napped again while I studied. All the problems slowly worked themselves out. But the transaction was settled: I belonged to God.

I'll use a biblical image to explain what I mean. Ancient Hebrews could sell themselves for six years to other Jews, after that they received their freedom. Then God made another provision: "But suppose your servant says, 'I will not leave you,' because he loves you and your family, and he has done well with you. In that case, take an awl and push it through his earlobe into the door. After that, he will be your servant for life. And do the same for your female servants" (Deuteronomy 15:16–17).

Whenever I read those words and think of the slave's branding, I do a fast-forward and think of Jesus' pierced hands and feet as his mark of servitude to God.

Then I think of myself. I don't have any physical markings to show the ownership of God. Even so, I belong to God. God is my owner. I have voluntarily sold myself into divine slavery.

For those of us who are owned by God, we seek our Owner's will through prayer. By deliberate choice, we turn over the decisions to our Owner. If we contemplate that, it gives us peace. We no longer need to worry, because our needs are in the hands of our Owner.

> And remember, if you were a slave when the Lord called you, you are now free in the Lord. And if you were free when the Lord called you, you are now a slave of Christ. God paid a high price for you, so don't be enslaved by the world (1 Corinthians 7:22–23).

Owner God,
remind me that I belong to you forever,
and you'll never let me go. Amen.

Chapter Twelve
My Master

I love the portion of prayer from the *Book of Common Worship* that reads:

We have followed too much the devices and desires of our own hearts. We have offended against Thy holy laws. We have left undone those things which we ought to have done; and we have done those things which we ought not to have done; and there is no health in us. But Thou, O Lord, have mercy upon us, miserable offenders.

Doesn't that sound like the humble way a wayward servant might approach his or her master? It's not merely a prayer of, "Father, forgive me because I've sinned." When I think of God as the Master, this is one of the prayers that fit that situation: I have gone my own way and have not done the will of my Master.

Perhaps I think of that prayer because of the poetic flow of the words; maybe because in the past I heard them often in church. More likely it's because the words graphically describe my lack of faithfulness to God's service.

I *am* often a wayward slave. Too often I have known the right thing to do and yet have chosen the path of disobedience. I'm not talking about what we consider the major sins. In fact, the more faithfully we serve the Master, the more aware we become of failing in little, almost insignificant ways.

Do I need a ball of fire from heaven to tell me, "Speak evil of no one?" Can't I be aware of it simply because I know what the Master wants from me? Don't I know that when I act less than lovingly toward the driver who cuts me off on the expressway, I'm showing my faithlessness as a servant?

Sometimes I hang my head and cry out, "I'm a miserable servant. I have failed." Or I repeat the words quoted above. They bring comfort, especially when I repeat the entire prayer that concludes with these sentences:

Spare Thou those, O God, who confess their faults. Restore Thou those who are penitent, according to Thy promises declared unto mankind in Christ Jesus our Lord. And grant, O most merciful Father, for His sake; that we may hereafter live a godly, righteous, and sober life; to the glory of Thy holy name. Amen.

Then I know, once again, I have been forgiven. The Master has looked on his slave and said, "I have mercy on you when you couldn't have mercy on others."

That's one picture inside my head of God the Master. But I have another. Sometimes when I pray, I speak freely with the Master who smiles at me and encourages me when I do the right thing. This is the voice that says, "Well done, good and faithful servant."

Some days I think of myself as bowing before my Master, knowing in my heart that I have served as faithfully as I've understood how. Yet it's often difficult for me to hear the voice say, "Well done." Too many years in association with those who want to keep me lowly and in my place bring the mocking words, "Ah, that's pride speaking. You're not humble if you think you deserve to hear the Master say you've done well. Even at your best, you're still not good enough."

Yet God exhorts us to faithfulness. Only God knows whether or when we measure up. Wouldn't it be a sad situation if we heard from God only such words as, "Miserable offender. Repent or perish!"?

I like to think of God as a kind Master. By that I don't mean an old softie or someone to manipulate, but a God who smiles at me when I do the right thing: when I treat someone else the way I want to be treated; when I do a spontaneous act of kindness; when I sincerely listen to a troubled friend. In those instances, I don't think it's pride that allows me to hear the words, "Well done."

In fact, as I've pursued the mental image of God the Master, this is the aspect I see more and more. This view comes out in the parable Jesus told of the three servants whose master gave them various sums of money and then went away (see Matthew 25:14–30). One servant received five talents—a weight of gold of immense value. The second received two, and the third received only one.

Too many of us who know the parable tend to equate ourselves with the third servant. But if I've grasped my Bible correctly, the general context says that Jesus told that parable for the benefit of the Pharisees and scribes—the insufferable, self-righteous leaders of his day.

The parable tells us that when the master returned, he found two of his servants had pleased him by faithfully investing his money, because they understood what the master wanted them to do. "The master was full of praise. 'Well done, my good and faithful servant. You have been faithful in handling this small amount, so now I will give you many more responsibilities. Let's celebrate together!'" (v. 21).

That's where I find comfort when I pray as the servant before my Master. "God, I've done the best I know how," I say. "To you, I bring the results of my service." I can hear myself saying those words after I have taught a Sunday school class, ushered at church, or donated food to the homeless shelter. Am I—at that moment—the "miserable offender"? I think not.

I like to consider myself God's love slave. I have voluntarily taken on servitude to God for the entirety of my life. And, frankly, I'd be a little crazy in the head to serve a God who does little but tell me how sinful I am, how often I fail, or how often I need to repent.

I love my service to God because I know my life pleases him. Oops, some finger-pointing moralists are going to get me for that. I still need the admonishment of the Master's voice. But I've had much of that in my life; now I'm enjoying a relationship in which I believe I often please God.

In this master-servant relationship, I think of a provision made in the Old Testament. God provided that Hebrews could sell themselves into indentured bondage to another Hebrew for six years. The seventh year, the masters were told to set the slaves free and "... do not send him away empty-handed. Give him a generous farewell gift from your flock, your threshing floor, and your winepress" (Deuteronomy 15:13–14).

The rest of the command to which I referred in the previous chapter can then be seen in a whole new light. "But suppose your servant says, 'I will not leave you,' because he loves you and your family, and he has done well with you. In that case, take an awl and push it through his earlobe into the door. After that, he will be your servant for life. And do the same for your female servants" (vv. 16–17).

Those indentured servants could choose to remain slaves. It was a choice, and they made it because they loved their master. I'm one of those love slaves. God has done more for me than bore a hole in my ear. God has put the mark of the crucifixion in my heart. I belong to God, and I serve my Master joyfully and willingly.

And now, Israel, what does the LORD your God require of you? He requires only that you fear the LORD your God, and live in a way that pleases him, and love him and serve him with all your heart and soul. And you must always obey the LORD's commands and decrees that I am giving you today for your own good (Deuteronomy 10:12–13).

Master of my life,
as I bow before you
and give account of my servanthood,
may I hear your voice say,
"You're a good and faithful servant.
Come and share in my happiness." Amen.

Chapter Thirteen
The Lowly Servant

"Saved to serve." The red-lettered banner proclaimed the theme of the six-day conference where I was one of the speakers. The taxi driver helped me carry my bulky suitcase and two large boxes of books inside.

After I registered, the director told me the motel was "just down the street a little ways." I had seen the motel sign on the way in; it was a mile away, down a heavily traveled four-lane highway.

"Could someone drive me?" I asked and pointed to the boxes.

"It's not *that* far," she said and turned away from me. Feeling helpless, I looked around. Several people with name tags chatted and drank coffee. I looked their way, hoping one of them would see my dilemma and carry at least one box. I didn't know any of them or feel comfortable in asking, so I picked up my load. Once loaded, I asked a man to open the door for me, but he didn't offer any further help.

As I trudged down the road in the July heat, I thought of the conference theme. It made me wonder what the people had in mind with such words as "saved to serve." Couldn't those participants see my obvious need for help?

By the time I reached the motel, I was thinking about how I might have reacted. I like to help others—especially when it's easy, pleasant, or convenient. Many of us do. But too often in churches and volunteer organizations, we take on the prestigious tasks, but become remarkably busy with other things when the "grunt work" comes around.

This situation isn't unique to our culture or time. I thought of an incident that took place on the night of Jesus' betrayal. Passover had begun, so being good Jews, Jesus and his disciples ate the special meal that Thursday evening. The one glitch in the scenario was the foot-washing bit.

In wealthy households, the lowest servant had the task of foot-washing. People walked on dusty roads with only sandals on their feet. They had no way to approach a house with clean feet. Someone had the task of taking off the sandals, washing the dirty feet, and drying them.

The prelude to Jesus taking on the role of the lowly servant reads like this: "... Jesus knew that his hour had come to leave this world and return to his Father. He had loved his disciples during his ministry on earth, and now he loved them to the very end" (John 13:1).

The story unfolds. None of the disciples had been willing to act as the lowly foot-washer, so apparently they were prepared to eat with filthy feet. Without grumbling and without rebuke, Jesus gets up from the meal, pours water into a basin, wraps a towel around his waist, and kneels before each of the twelve disciples.

Peter, to his credit, has enough sense to say, "No, you can't wash my feet." He acknowledges that it isn't right for the teacher to wash the pupils' feet. The book of John gives no indication that the others objected.

Jesus offers Peter a spiritual lesson about cleansing and then goes on to wash the others. When he finishes, Jesus asks, "Do you understand what I was doing?" (v. 12). Without waiting for their reply, he hammers home the truth: "You call me 'Teacher' and 'Lord,' and you are right, because that's what I am. And since I, your Lord and Teacher, have washed your feet, you ought to wash each other's feet. I have given you an example to follow. Do as I have done to you" (vv. 15–16).

This story—even though it covers only seventeen verses—reverses roles for us. I imagine those brief moments as a disciple: I'm the master and Jesus is the servant. How do I handle that? How do I think of Jesus, the Lord of Lords and King of Kings, and look upon him as a servant, even for the briefest moment?

As I contemplate that concept, I have to laugh. Why, it's really easy. I do it all the time, I think. I'm quite skilled at telling God how to do things. In my times of grandiosity, I have it all figured out for God; the Divine One needs only to follow the instructions I've formulated inside my head.

Peter didn't like it when Jesus took on the role of a servant, but he consented, because he understood the point Jesus was making. He acted out the role of servanthood for us, teaching us by example.

Now, how does this work in prayer? How do I turn to Jesus, the lowly servant, and pray? After trying to imagine myself as the master and Jesus as the servant, I thought of my limitations of wisdom and understanding. How could I dare to direct Jesus to do something when I can't see beyond the immediate results of my requests? What makes me think I could issue even the slightest command that wouldn't throw the proverbial wrench into the universe's machinery?

And yet, for those moments, two thousand years ago, Jesus knelt before twelve different men, one of whom left shortly afterward to betray him. The other eleven ran away when danger came. Still, Jesus says to them, "I'm the head honcho, but for now I've become the lowly servant."

In my search to figure out how to make contact in prayer with Jesus, the lowly servant, I finally got the message. First, I can't do it. Second, it's not what God wants me to do.

In fact, the end of the story in John's Gospel quotes these words of Jesus: "I tell you the truth, slaves are not greater than their master. Nor is the messenger more important than the one who sends the message. Now that you know these things, God will bless you for doing them" (vv. 16–17).

My practical, day-to-day problem is that I continue to get the roles reversed. I tell God, "Take away the pain," or "God, open the door for me."

God wants us to ask. All through both Old and New Testaments, God tells (commands!) us to do just that. The problem is that we tend to take it a step further and tell (Insist? Demand? *Command?*) God to do things.

During my struggle with this idea, it has helped me to read some works of the English Puritans. I recall being struck by their prayers. Not only did they have a powerful sense of reverence for God, but when they prayed, they used a phrase that I liked: "May it please you to …"

They were making their requests known to God and adding that they wanted their requests answered, but only if it pleased God to do so. Perhaps our prayers *imply* such an attitude. I'm not sure mine always do. But meditating on John 13 has forced me to reexamine and monitor my praying.

I hear myself asking, "Am I treating God as the lowly servant or am I aware that as the lowly servant, I have no rights? That I own nothing except what God is pleased to give me? Am I usurping the role of master and asking God to serve me?"

Each time my thoughts move in that direction, I conclude with, "Forgive me, Lord."

"You are my servant." For I have chosen you and will not throw you away. Don't be afraid, for I am with you. Don't be discouraged, for I am your God (Isaiah 41:9–10).

Master of my life,
remind me of our relationship.
It pleases you when I ask;
now help me not to try to run the world for you,
not even to run my own life. Amen.

Chapter Fourteen
The Lawgiver

On the chalkboard for my Sunday school class I drew a small square inside a large circle. "The circle represents life and the box stands for the laws of God. Where are you?" I placed an X inside the box and I placed another outside the box. "Which best represents you and your understanding of the laws of God?"

From there I went on to explain that committed Christians tend to take one of two positions: inside or outside the box. Those inside the box are keenly aware of God's laws and carefully obey them. Their lives revolve around staying away from the four walls of the box. Their freedom, although limited, is that they can do what they want, but within the confines of the walls.

Some in the class used the box to define their lives. The laws, rules, regulations, injunctions, commands, and statutes of God were about as far as they would travel.

"It's almost like I'd have to ask God about doing anything for fear it would be wrong," someone commented.

Those who saw themselves outside the box were the ones who said, "Life is free and unrestricted. We can do anything we want, except those things in that tiny little box over there."

One member of the class said, "I've always thought the Ten Commandments were there to free us, not restrict us. To me, they say, 'You can do anything you want, except for these ten things.'"

In contrast to this positive view, my mother was one of those people who held a negative view: The world was getting worse, everything in the world was sinful, and the only hope was to regard everything around us as evil. She regularly quoted 1 John 2:15–17:

Do not love this world nor the things it offers you, for when you love the world, you do not have the love of the Father in you. For the world offers only a craving for physical pleasure, a craving for everything we see, and pride in our achievements and possessions. These are not from the Father, but are from this world. And this world is fading away, along with everything that people crave. But anyone who does what pleases God will live forever.

A legalistic Christian, Mom had a long list of don'ts. While still a teenager, and tired of hearing her negatives, I asked, "I know all the things you don't do and can't do, but what do you do that's fun or enjoyable?"

"I go to church. I read my Bible. I talk to my friends."

"Some fun," I said. Her negative attitude is part of the reason I had no interest in the Christian faith when I was young.

Then, about twenty years ago, I had a new insight from reading the book of Psalms. Many of the psalms praise God for creation of the mountains, skies, sea, and land. The poets extol God for giving us hills and valleys, and fertile land. How could that be all bad?

Gradually, I began to think of life differently. According to the Old Testament poets, God created a beautiful and bountiful world for us to embrace and care for. I could enjoy the fruits of divine creation without feeling guilty or negative. Or, to use my earlier image, I could stay outside the box.

I love the world God has given me to live in. And when I think of those oft-quoted verses from 1 John, it seems to me the context defines the writer's intentions. He wasn't talking about life in general, but the worldly system of his day, the attitudes that opposed God. On the positive side, John was talking about loving one another and keeping God's commandments.

God is the Lawgiver and has prescribed behavior for us to live harmoniously and happily. This Lawgiver is compassionate and understanding. Psalm 103:13–15 gives me this picture: "The LORD is like a father to his children, tender and compassionate to those who fear him. For he knows how weak we are; he remembers we are only dust. Our days on earth are like grass; like wildflowers, we bloom and die."

That's the kind of God I see as the Lawgiver, not someone out there to "get us" or to run us in when we break a rule. God's laws guide us—gently, whenever possible. It seems to me that God has tried to make it easy for us to understand the right way to live, but we keep making it hard on ourselves by adding to the laws.

For instance, once Jesus confronted the top Jewish leaders of his day over the matter of the Sabbath law, which said they could not work on that day. The hungry disciples had plucked grain and eaten it. Then Jesus said to them, "The Sabbath was made to meet the needs of people, and not people to meet the requirements of the Sabbath" (Mark 2:27).

That's the Lawgiver saying, "Live in this world and enjoy it. Praise me as the one who frees you to live the abundant life." The divine laws set us free to embrace love, joy, peace, longsuffering, kindness, goodness, faithfulness, gentleness, and self-control. See Galatians 5:23, where the apostle Paul adds, "There is no law against these things!"

> I have rejoiced in your laws as much as in riches. I will delight in your decrees and not forget your word (Psalm 119:14, 16).

REVITALIZE YOUR PRAYER LIFE

Eternal Giver of Laws,
your divine laws are for us,
for our health and safety,
for growth and well-being.
Teach us to see them as examples of your loving kindness
rather than restrictions on life. Amen.

Chapter Fifteen
My Lawyer

Jesus is our advocate, or lawyer, before God. For many, this image conjures up a negative view of God.

Many have little trouble grasping Jesus as the loving, committed attorney out to defend us before a just and angry God who wants to condemn us all to eternal damnation. Because of Jesus, the Judge doesn't—but he really wants to.

Why not think of God as a loving judge, one who wants to free humanity, but has to have a reason to do so?

The apostle Paul writes: "God presented him [Jesus Christ] as a sacrifice of atonement, through faith in his blood. He did this to demonstrate his justice, because in his forbearance he had left the sins committed beforehand unpunished—he did it to demonstrate his justice at the present time, so as to be just and the one who justifies those who have faith in Jesus" (Romans 3:25–26, NIV).

Those key words, "the just and the one who justifies"—or, for me, a better way to say it is, "the Righteous One and the One Who Makes Righteous"—make the point. God's justness (or justice) demands punishment for sin—that's basic. But God doesn't stop with that. Now the Judge turns around and finds a way to justify, or make right with him, those who believe in Jesus Christ.

Jesus isn't trying to placate an angry God on our behalf. As our lawyer, he's interceding on our behalf.

I like the concept of Jesus as my Lawyer.

After watching hundreds of lawyer shows on TV, I envision Jesus before the Holy Judge. When he enters our plea for any of our sins, of course, it's guilty. Where he goes to work for us is in the mitigating circumstances.

Jesus never defends our wrongdoing. He makes no excuses for us and allows none. "Guilty as charged" is the only possible response. Unlike us, he doesn't allow us to blame others for our circumstances or insist that we didn't know what we were doing.

Even though it doesn't work in our American justice system, Jesus' advocacy for us is simple. He asks for God to drop the charges. And the Righteous Judge listens, eager for a reason to do just that.

"The reason for my request," Jesus says, "is that I have never sinned. Accept my innocence in payment for his (or her) guilt."

It may not make legal sense, but it is a spiritual principle at work. Jesus himself never sinned, even though we have sinned regularly and repeatedly. He put us in right standing with the Great Judge by taking our guilt on himself.

That's pretty basic theology. Yet as I prayed today, it spoke to me in a new way. He's not trying to deny or clear my record by anything except his own intercession, by giving of himself.

And Jesus said, "Neither do I [condemn you]. Go and sin no more" (John 8:11).

"Neither do I condemn you," I hear Jesus say. "Go and sin no more" I don't understand the reasoning, the love and compassion, but I understand the words.

Now I seek to "sin no more."

> My dear children, I am writing this to you so that you will not sin. But if anyone does sin, we have an advocate who pleads our case before the Father. He is Jesus Christ, the one who is truly righteous. He himself is the sacrifice that atones for our sins—and not only our sins but the sins of all the world (1 John 2:1–2).

*My Special Lawyer,
you have given yourself to defend me,
to make me right before God.
How awesome!
How wonderful that you care that much.
Thank you. Amen.*

Chapter Sixteen
My Powerful Judge

I had sinned. Despite my efforts to convince myself that I hadn't really failed God, guilt whispered quietly, and then more loudly when I ignored its protests. It didn't matter if anyone else was aware. *I knew.* That self-knowledge made it terrible to bear.

During that period, I read every day from the Psalms. Although I didn't speak quite as dramatically as the poet, I understood his words on an emotional level: "When I refused to confess my sin, my body wasted away, and I groaned all day long. Day and night your hand of discipline was heavy on me. My strength evaporated like water in the summer heat" (Psalm 32:3–4).

I had sinned.

To make it worse, it wasn't what the Old Testament refers to as a sin of ignorance. I had deliberately gone astray. Before I sinned, I told myself that I was protecting my rights, standing up for myself and being faithful to my convictions. At other times, I've told myself that I had technically sinned, but I had really been overwhelmed by temptation (as though that made it a lesser offense).

The point is, I had sinned.

No matter how much I tried to push that truth away from myself, it refused to vanish. Finally, I gave up trying. Once I stripped away the self-deceptions and bowed my head before God, I admitted, "God, I have rebelled. I knowingly, willfully failed you."

As I came into the Divine Presence, the guilt overwhelmed me. Like David of old, I wailed, "Against you, and you alone, have I sinned; I have done what is evil in your sight. You will be proved right in what you say, and your judgment against me is just" (Psalm 51:4). I prayed that way even though my actions had hurt others—some of them indirectly. Right then, I committed myself to make things right with them later.

I couldn't focus on others at that moment, though, because ultimately, it was against the Powerful God of heaven that I had sinned. My immediate concern involved my relationship with God. In my mind, I saw myself standing with bowed head before the Powerful Judge who sees all and knows all.

I'm ready for the Judge to pronounce the sentence. What do I do now? Should I say anything? Remain silent? Once I would have perceived God as the one whose eyes swept across the land, watching me at every turn, ready to leap in front of me, and with pointed index finger, cry out, "You are the guilty man!"

Today, I think of God the Powerful Judge from the perspective of Romans 8:1–2: "So now there is no condemnation for those who belong to Christ Jesus. And because you belong to him, the power of the life-giving Spirit has freed you from the power of sin that leads to death."

Those two verses make me feel as if I am in front of the bench and the Powerful Judge has spoken those liberating words to me. Joy fills my heart! The Powerful Judge says I won't be punished!

This is in such contrast with the idea of judgment with punishment I used to have: "commit-the-crime-and-pay-the-penalty" kind of living. I wouldn't want to deny that aspect. After all, I am responsible for the wrongs I do and must face the consequences of my actions.

Yet God the Powerful Judge is so much more merciful.

In my student days at seminary, I learned that the basis for the Greek word *judge* means "to set in order." It can eventuate in punishment, corrective action, or an admonition. When God sets us in order, it's so that we don't have to live in a state of punishment or have a "G" for guilty engraved on our foreheads for the world to see.

The Powerful Judge makes us aware of our wrongdoing or our wrong attitude. We lower our eyes as we approach God's pureness and holiness. The closer we get, the more acutely we grasp our sinfulness. Then we stop and repeat the wail of Isaiah, who saw his sinfulness in contrast to the holiness of

God: "I have filthy lips, and I live among a people with filthy lips" (see Isaiah 6:5).

"I'm too wicked to come close to you," is what my heart used to cry out. Yet since I turned Romans 8:1–2 into a personal experience, I approach God differently.

"You have broken my eternal laws," I can hear the Powerful Judge say. "How do you plead?"

"Guilty," I say, saddened by the stupidity of what I've done. "And please, your honor, I want to say I'm sorry."

As that scene stays before me, I hear the Powerful Judge say, "Guilty as charged. Now, child, go, and sin no more."

The Powerful Judge may tell me that Someone has paid my fine, or I may hear, "Who can stand against you when I am on your side? Nothing can separate you from my love, which I show you in Christ Jesus."

Instead of dread, I can now face the Powerful Judge with peace.

God is the Powerful Judge, chastening us when we need it, prodding us when we deserve it, but the purpose is to get our feet walking straight and staying straight. God is not only a Powerful Judge, but the Powerful, *Loving* Judge.

As we pray, we not only confess our failures, but we give thanks to God that those sins are now out of our lives. The Powerful Judge has set them aside with these words, "Go and sin no more."

⚜ ⚜ ⚜

So now there is no condemnation for those who belong to Christ Jesus. And because you belong to him, the power of the life-giving Spirit has freed you from the power of sin that leads to death.... So God did what the law could not do. He sent his own Son in a body like the bodies we sinners have. And in that body God declared an end to sin's control over us by giving his Son as a sacrifice for our sins (Romans 8:1–3).

Powerful Judge of All Life,
forgive me because I have sinned against you.
Forgive me for losing sight of right living
and compassion,
and for not loving others the way I love myself.
Powerful Judge,
I accept your forgiveness with joyful thanksgiving. Amen.

Chapter Seventeen
My Favorite Teacher

"Watch out if you get Miss Linder," a boy in fifth grade said. "She's the meanest teacher in the school." I was in third grade then and didn't worry about Miss Irma Linder. But when I entered fifth grade, I was assigned to her class.

She was tough. Mean. Demanding. She had eyes that saw everything we did, even with her back to us. But despite it all, Miss Linder was my favorite teacher in grade school. I learned more from her than any of the others. She had a way of making me want to learn. When I did less than my best, I had the feeling that I had let her down as much as I had let myself down.

Since then, I've had other teachers I've loved or admired. But there's no question about my all-time, lifelong favorite teacher. His name is Jesus. Even his enemies called him "teacher" (rabbi) and recognized his great skill of communicating truth to his hearers.

When I talk to my Favorite Teacher, I hear myself begin sentence after sentence with, "Teach me...." Those are sincere words and express my heart's desire. I want to learn and I believe my Favorite Teacher wants me to learn.

One problem is that I want all the knowledge and the understanding *right now*. However, it just doesn't work that way in education. Like any top-quality teacher, Jesus instructs us slowly, methodically, and carefully.

My attitude reminds me of the time I learned the keyboard. I took typing in tenth grade, in the days before computers came into the classroom. The first class period, our teacher taught us typewriter basics, and before the session ended, we had our first chance to hit the keys. She made us use the small finger on either hand—our weakest fingers—and type half a page of nothing but *a; a; a; a;*. After mistakes and laughter at not being able to give the fingers enough pressure, we learned two more letters. Using the ring finger on both hands, we soon typed a half-page of *a;sl a;sl a;sl a;sl.*

By the end of the class, typing the same four letters bored me. Worse, they weren't even words. I wanted to type real words and sentences. The wise teacher, anticipating our attitude, urged us to resist. "Learn the keyboard right and you'll become fast and accurate typists," she told us.

I didn't like it, but I did it her way. For weeks, we struggled through the entire keyboard. To make it worse, in our classes, we didn't have the letters on the keys, so it was truly typing by feeling the keys.

I've now been typing so many years that my fingers dance across the keys automatically. I don't think about hitting an *a* or an *f*, I just type. It's automatic because I learned to do it the right way.

The parallels are probably obvious. We start small, and we learn step by step. We develop proficiency as we grasp and assimilate the lessons Jesus has for us. Then we move on to more complex lessons.

Occasionally, I have to remind myself that I'm the pupil and Jesus is the teacher. I forget and instruct him about how to run the universe, how to take care of my family and my friends, or at least how to structure my life.

Most days, however, I sincerely feel I'm an apt pupil. I've been sensitive to my Favorite Teacher's instructions and obeyed implicitly. On my bad days, it's not so much that I don't want to learn, but I just don't seem to get the lesson.

Even when I don't get what I'm supposed to learn, I can come to the Teacher for help. I want to learn, but I don't want to keep typing *a;sl*. I want to rush into the big stuff and have him explain everything to me.

That's often where my spiritual learning curve takes a downward spiral. I can't understand the divine rationale for what's going on. I ask questions, and sometimes I get an answer, but more often, there's no response.

I've begun to figure out the matter of silence. For instance, when I pray for my Favorite Teacher to teach me how to live a godly life more perfectly, what I really mean is, "Teacher, make it easy for me."

What I don't mean is, "Teacher, make me figure it out for myself. Stay at my elbow, but make me do the work." The reality is that God wants the latter for me. Some of my biggest learning spurts have come when I'm totally confused. I can't figure out what to do next. Sometimes I feel angry or irritated because my Favorite Teacher isn't feeding me answers. I don't like doing all the work myself.

I think of Peter from time to time. He got instructions from Jesus along with a few promises. Jesus promised that Peter would strengthen the other apostles, that he would be a rock, and even told him how he would die. But he never laid out all the teachings for him in six easy lessons. And Peter didn't have a perfect learning record either.

Despite the man's ups and downs, the Teacher didn't give up on him. He kept working with him, pushing him when he wasn't ready and nudging him when he needed it.

Most of us are like Peter. Some of the lessons our Favorite Teacher wants us to grasp we pick up on immediately. But other insights don't come in a day or even over a period of months. Some are lessons we learn only after years of following Jesus. We never graduate from the School of Godliness.

Even though we don't understand all the reasons for our mess-ups on many of the lessons, Jesus is the Favorite Teacher. He loves us and wants us to learn, enough that he won't give up on us. His word to us is, "Come to me ... learn from me."

When we respond and pray, "Teach me what I need to know," Jesus hears us. Those two words alone, "Teach me," please the Teacher because he likes eager pupils.

> Teach me your decrees, O LORD;
> I will keep them to the end (Psalm 119:33).
>
> Teach me your ways, O LORD, that I may live according to your truth! Grant me purity of heart, so that I may honor you (Psalm 27:11).

My Favorite Teacher,
make me an eager pupil,
encourage me to learn,
and thanks for not giving up on me. Amen.

Chapter Eighteen
My Best Friend

Friends play an important role in my life. It's hard for me to think of a period when I didn't have several close ones.

My best friend is David. The close relationship we have didn't happen merely because of the passage of time, although that certainly played a role. In analyzing our friendship, the most significant factor has been that we nurtured the relationship. We spent time together. We talked. We shared things about ourselves that we had told no one else. I share this about David because it's the best way I know to talk about my Best Friend in the universe. His name is Jesus.

This morning, I went for a walk with him through a wooded area near my home. I had a quiet, peaceful time. Of course, I did most of the talking, because Jesus is a better listener than I am. But I paused occasionally. A few times I stopped, and we pushed aside our conversation to take in the wild ducks that live all year long at the little lake. Jesus and I sat in silence on a bench as I stared at the murky water and gazed upward at the cloudless sky. In the far distance, I heard a child call another. Although I couldn't see them, cars occasionally whizzed down the nearby street.

Even in the silence, I was aware of my Friend's presence. In fact, we didn't always need words. Once I closed my eyes and "felt" him give me a warm, lingering embrace.

"I can tell you anything," I said. "You're the only person who already knows everything about me and I don't have to censor my thoughts or feelings."

I like to think he smiled then.

This morning, as I concentrated on my special friendship with Jesus, again I compared it to my relationship with David. I love my friend, and we've told each other many times of our mutual affection and commitment. My relationship with David is the closest human friendship I have. I trust David. He knows things about me others don't know. In fact, I have told him he fits my definition of a perfect friend: someone who knows everything about me, still loves me, and has no plan for my self-improvement.

Jesus doesn't quite fit that definition. True, he knows everything about me *and* he knows it before I do. As it says in Psalm 139:4, "You know what I am going to say even before I say it, LORD."

Jesus still loves me, despite the wickedness of my thoughts. Despite the disreputable lusts and yearnings that flow through my heart, he doesn't love me less. "You know my heart, Jesus," I say from time to time. But I say that for Cec, not for him, to remind myself that even though the garbage of my mind may be four feet deep and increasing, it doesn't diminish his love for me.

"I'm your friend, and I'm here to listen. Tell me everything." Although not spoken audibly, these words are part of the image I have of my friend Jesus.

The one big difference between my Best Friend and other friends in my life is that Jesus *does* have a plan for my self-improvement. He constantly pushes me toward a life of holiness.

Today, when Jesus and I walked together, I remembered a poster I had seen in a Sunday school classroom a few years ago. It showed Jesus with his hand on the shoulder of a young boy, and they were walking together. From the animated expression on the boy's face, I knew they were having a delightful time together. That's my idea of friendship with Jesus—simply enjoying each other's presence.

Sometimes when I walk with my Best Friend, I suddenly become aware that not only am I doing all the talking, I'm not even giving Jesus a chance to answer.

Once in a while (not often), I walk in silence and I try to think of him. Sometimes I meditate on some of the words in the Bible that he spoke. Or maybe I ask him to help me live out a statement such as, "Don't let your hearts be troubled. Trust in God, and trust also in me" (John 14:1). Other times, I simply rejoice in being in his presence. Or I may talk to him about the people I care for deeply and who need his help.

My friendship isn't always smooth and simple. Not long ago, we had an argument, Jesus and I. Okay, I did the arguing and he did the listening. I had asked him for something specific, something that would, in my thinking, make me a better person and a stronger Christian. I prayed and searched my heart for my motive. I was sure Jesus would answer yes.

I didn't get what I asked for, and I was angry.

"I'm going for a walk," I told my wife that day. "I feel the Lord let me down, and I have to get it straightened out."

Jesus got an earful of complaints, groanings, and rantings. For perhaps twenty minutes, I walked along and complained. The anger seethed. "You let me down," I said. "I know I fail all the time, but you're not supposed to do that."

Jesus never answered me, but he didn't leave me or rebuke me.

After a while, I felt as if he were asking, "Is it all out of your system now?"

"Yes, it's okay," I said, "even though I still think my idea was better."

He's my Best Friend. He doesn't mind if I talk that way. I don't have a happy ending to that story. No miracles. No chance to reverse it so that I got what I wanted. Jesus didn't explain a thing to me—and I'm not sure he ever will. But it's okay.

It's okay because he loves me. It's okay because he knows what's best for me—even when I still don't understand.

After that particular incident, while I brooded, I had to run to the drugstore. There I saw a little girl and her mother. The girl kept begging her mother to buy her something, and the woman kept saying no or shaking her head.

"Why not?" the little girl demanded, hands on her hips.

"Because I said no, and that's all I need to tell you right now."

That incident sent me back to my Best Friend. "I'm sorry. I'm not apologizing for not accepting your decision as best for me. With my limited wisdom, I still think I should have gotten what I asked for. But I heard you speak to me through that mother. You said no, and that's all I need to understand right now." Then came peace.

Because Jesus is the Best Friend of all believers, we can open our hearts to him and tell him anything. Our Best Friend walks with us, cares deeply for us, and wants only good things for us.

> [Jesus said,] "You are my friends if you do what I command. I no longer call you slaves, because a master doesn't confide in his slaves. Now you are my friends, since I have told you everything the Father told me. You didn't choose me. I chose you.

I appointed you to go and produce lasting fruit" (John 15:14–16).

My dear friend Jesus,
you're the best friend I've ever had or ever will have.
I'm safe and comfortable with you.
You won't let me down, betray me, or hurt me.
Please help me be a faithful friend to you.
You deserve my best after all you've done for me. Amen.

Chapter Nineteen
The Miracle Worker

Miracles! Think of the range of them in the Bible.

The waters parted at the Red Sea and again at the Jordan River.

Elisha made a metal axe head float in the water.

Sarah and Elizabeth had babies long after the menopausal years.

For forty years, God supplied a food called manna to the Israelites as they trekked across the land.

Peter was locked in prison and an angel unlocked the doors and freed him.

Jesus turned plain drinking water into first-class, grade-A wine.

What about the healing miracles? The first miracle Mark records is Jesus' healing of a man with a withered arm. (See Mark 3:1–4.) After hemorrhaging for twelve years, a woman was healed by Jesus. Peter's mother-in-law received a healing touch. Jesus restored sight to Bartimaeus.

Some of the healings are what I call mental healings. These were people with unclean or evil spirits who were "restored" (the usual biblical word) to normalcy after meeting Jesus or one of the apostles.

So why don't we see the rash of healings today when holy men and women pass through town? Miracles like the sun not moving for twenty-four hours, or mental hospitals being cleared out?

I wouldn't even try to answer, but I'm convinced God still pulls off a few miracles. Or maybe even more of them than we realize. Maybe we need to think of miracles anytime we pray, "God, will you do this?"

That's the real test, isn't it? When we need something and we ask for divine intervention, we're asking for a miracle. The word *intervene* is what makes it a miracle. Looked at this way, don't most of us pray for (and receive) miracles every day?

Here's an incident of divine intervention. I left the church at age ten and didn't look back for a decade. Only later did I learn that my elderly Sunday school teacher, Marie Garbie, prayed for my conversion. "Of all the children who went through my classes, you were the one most on my heart. Not one day did I ever miss praying for you," she later told me.

Mrs. Garbie prayed every single day for more than ten years for God to *intervene* in my life. She asked God to step in front of me and block the wrong road. Finally, God answered her prayers.

From my perspective, I have no idea what made me turn to God, except I was at a place where I felt the emptiness of life and began to ask, "Is this all there is?" For reasons I can't explain—nor care to try—I sensed I would find the answer in God. For Mrs. Garbie, however, the answer was simple: "God gave me the miracle I asked for."

God intervenes in many ways. One problem is that we don't know when it gets classified as a miracle and when it would have happened anyway.

Let's say I need a job. I apply at a company and eventually get interviewed. I pray, "God, if this is the right job, let the interview go well." It goes well. Then I pray again, "If this is the right job, let them offer it to me." I get the job. Did God intervene and give me the job? Or what if I don't get the job? Is that the intervention of God that says, "Well, child, this really isn't what I want for you?"

Answer: For me, it's a matter of faith. I pray, I believe, and God answers. That's a miracle. That faith leads me to pray to the Miracle Worker to intervene in dozens of ways, such as in work situations, in relationships, or with financial problems.

At times I don't get an answer. I simply walk on, moving from left foot to right, and I trust God to clear the trail for me as I get there. On other occasions, I hear God speaking through what I call the Inner Voice.

For instance, a publisher once called me about writing a celebrity's biography. He had read books by twelve experienced writers and had narrowed it to six who might author the biography; I was one of the six. I prayed for God to intervene. A few of my friends would have told me to add, "... if it's your will." I assumed that it was God's will for me, so I prayed that it would happen.

I received a call. "We're down to two people, and you're one of them."

After the phone call, I went wild with anticipation. But as I prayed, word came to me from the Inner Voice. "You have come in second."

I knew that voice. I didn't get the job. Although disappointed, I thanked God for an answer. (A week later I learned they asked the other writer.)

Some might call that a kind of reverse miracle, but it reminds me again of the Miracle Worker's intervention in our lives. God is there to do whatever is necessary for our growth.

Another way the Miracle Worker operates is through timing. At just the right moment something happens. A member of our Sunday school class, Judy Liedtke, was in the hospital and the doctor told her she had cancer. She began to cry, asking God to send her someone. Twelve miles away, my wife said, "I feel I need to call Judy."

Miracle? It was to Judy when she heard Shirley's voice on the phone. "God knew just when and who to send," were her first words.

Today, I often hear the word *synchronicity*. From the Greek, it combines "time" and "together." The term refers to those special moments when actions happen—seemingly at random—and yet if we're in tune with the Miracle Worker, we know it came at exactly the right moment.

Sometimes miracles come from behind the scenes. God is already rehearsing the show before we even know there's such a production scheduled. For example, most of us have had someone shove a book at us, saying, "You really need to read this." We get busy and stick it on the shelf. Then one day, for no apparent reason, we pick up the book. As we start to read, lights blaze, internal trumpets sound, and the fireworks sparkle. "Wow! This is a wonderful book," we say. "Just what I needed."

It was all in the timing. That's the miracle. Before we were ready to receive the answer, God provided it.

Miracles work through circumstances. One day I was teaching Sunday school and a woman walked in and sat down. Our lesson was on grief, and before long, she opened up to talk about a divorce she had just gone through and was still grieving over. Class members talked to her and she found great comfort in what they said.

Just before the class ended, I mentioned the name of our church.

"What? Is that where I am?" She thought she had gone to a church of her denomination two blocks away. As she wiped away tears, she said, "This lesson was just for me."

Why not call it a synchronistic miracle by the Miracle Worker of the Ages?

If we ponder the actions of the Miracle Worker, it offers us the wonderful assurance that God loves us enough to override the divinely enacted natural laws. I love the image of the all-seeing eyes of God, because it says the Miracle Worker never sleeps or takes a vacation. The eyes of God knows where we are at every moment. Sometimes we need protection or need a friend to listen. Or we may need solitude or relief from pain.

The Miracle Worker is the God who cares enough to provide. The provisions aren't always according to our specifications. We may pray for God to remove a headache and the Miracle Worker may quietly whisper, "Take an aspirin." Or the voice might say, "Relax. Get rid of the tension."

Most important, the Miracle Worker is present, always willing to listen, encouraging us to ask for divine intervention. Maybe we don't need more miracles as much as we need the ability to perceive those already around us. Maybe we need to think about the answers God is already giving us.

> You are the God of great wonders! You demonstrate your awesome power among the nations. Your road led through the sea, your pathway through the mighty waters—a pathway no one knew was there! (Psalm 77:14, 19).

Cecil Murphey

Miracle-Working God,
thank you for intervening in my life today and yesterday,
all the days of the past,
and all the days of the future.
Your love assures me that even when I pray foolishly
or erroneously,
you care and you still work miracles.
Thank you. Amen.

Chapter Twenty
The Divine Healer

About a dozen years ago, I began to apply Romans 12:1. It urges us to offer our *bodies* as living sacrifices to God. The apostle Paul also tells us twice in 1 Corinthians that our bodies are God's *temples*. He draws two powerful images: living sacrifices and temples.

To me that means God is concerned about us caring for and protecting our bodies. After all, our bodies are the essence of what we work with. Our minds may be more important, but they surely don't function independently. If our bodies aren't important, why would we have a resurrection that promises some form of physical substance?

Then why do we tend to discount the body or pay too little attention to its care? I've begun to realize the answer—for me, that is. If we acknowledge our responsibility to care for the temple of God, then we're held accountable for how we treat it. And if we misuse our bodies or offer God blemished sacrifices, what does that say about our commitment?

To start, I acknowledge I'm a temple abuser. I have offered my badly-taken-care-of and less-than-perfect body to God. For years, I was among the sleep-deprived generation. I ate a lot of foods that harmed my body. Until I faced some serious physical problems, I didn't think much about exercise. I allowed stress into my life when I could have found healthy ways to correct it.

I confess to all of those sins; I've battled physical illness as a result. *But* God, being ever merciful, allows us to bring our battered, torn, worn-out, and abused bodies to the place of prayer. We can talk to God about our health. We can ask for healing. I won't say we always get it, but I do believe it's available.

Although I've noticed them before, the words of Jesus in instances of individual healing have taken on new meaning for me. He heals and sometimes adds, "Go and sin no more."

What a tag-on that is! Is Jesus actually saying to us, "You have high blood pressure because you have mishandled your body?" "Your emphysema comes from your mistreating the holy temple of God?"

In most cases, I think so. I'm not writing this to bring condemnation to anyone. It's my personal attempt to come to grips with issues in my own life and to discover a fuller, richer commitment to the Healer of All Diseases.

For me, a fuller, richer life simply has to involve our bodies. We know the stereotype of the sweet, elderly woman who is confined to bed and spends her waking moments interceding for others. I wouldn't fit into that category.

When I'm sick, I am s-i-c-k. I don't do much except think about how miserable I am. I pray for healing and beg God to make me well so I can get back to my normal energy level. When I'm sick, I assure you, I do little praying for anyone other than poor Cec Murphey.

That then leads me to realize that when I pray for healing, I am asking the Divine Physician to make me healthy. If I'm healthy, I'm better able to be in touch with God's presence. My mind is not on my wretched condition and I can concentrate on other things.

I don't like to be sick. If I'm sick, I pray for healing. That part is fine, but it's not enough. Here's a theory I live with, but I wouldn't try to force it on anyone else. I believe that the Creator God made our bodies to serve us, and also to teach us.

When I was twenty years old, I tasted shrimp for the first time. It was also the last time. Within an hour, I was miserable and vomited. It would be stupid of me ever to eat shrimp again. My body taught me something. I believe our bodies talk to us all the time, but we don't always listen. They tell us when we're tired, but we boost ourselves with caffeine instead of resting (my confession again).

Here's the philosophy I now embrace: When I am sick, there is a reason. So I pray, "God, show me why I *need* to be sick." Bold? Crazy? Perhaps. In the past, it has been my unconscious way of dropping out of the action or pushing away pressure.

This awareness came into being when I was a pastor. Every year during December we had many festivities and special services at church that I attended, besides my own family functions. I took Communion to every shut-in. All adult Sunday school classes invited me to their Christmas parties. By the end of December, I was worn out.

Could I acknowledge my tiredness? Not me. I took a day off, and started pumping up again for the new year. Then I noticed that for five years in a row I came down with a nasty cold early in January. That cold was so bad that no matter what medication I took, I had to go to bed.

The sixth year it happened, I got the message. I had brought my physical sickness on myself. When I get sick, I need to listen to my body and ask the Divine Doctor, "What is happening that makes me need to be sick at this time?"

When I listen, it's amazing the answers I get. Unfortunately, I haven't always wanted to hear those answers. Part of my growth as a disciple of God is to ask God tough questions about myself and listen to the answers.

Do I call on the Healer? Without hesitation. However, when I pray, it's more than for just physical relief, it's also to help me understand what I've done to make my body this way. "Divine Healer, this is an issue of obedience," I say. "You're speaking, but I'm not hearing. Speak to me and help me hear what I need to know. Heal me and then enable me to go and sin no more."

As I pause to reflect on the Divine Healer, I feel such gratitude. Isn't it wonderful that God cares about every aspect of life? God doesn't limit divine intervention and interest to only "spiritual" things, because every facet of my life is spiritual.

That's where my prayers to the Divine Healer have led me. God wants to heal every part of me—the outer temple of the body as well as the inner temple of my mind and emotions.

We can pray to the Healer who is a caring, wonderful God.

> He said [the LORD], "If you will listen carefully to the voice of the LORD your God and do what is right in his sight, obeying his commands and keeping all his decrees, then I will not make you suffer any of the diseases I sent on the Egyptians; for I am the LORD who heals you" (Exodus 15:26).

Divine Physician,
heal all my diseases,
all my waywardness,
and all my hardness of heart,
so that I worship you in my body and in my inner being.
Thank you for caring about every part of my life. Amen.

Chapter Twenty-One
The Righteous One

Think about the messages we hear these days:
Jesus loves me, no matter what.
Jesus is there, always understanding.
Jesus will pick me up when I fall.
Are the above statements true?
Absolutely.

For at least the past decade, I've listened to sermon after sermon about how much Jesus loves us. We can't say too much about God's love and forgiveness. But too many such messages drip with sentimentality as if that's the total picture of God.

"Love, just love and nothing else; everything will be all right." Not only is that poor theology, but the words often make Jesus sound like a wimp. It may be true that even when we abuse him, ignore him, chase him away when he doesn't like what we're doing or saying or temporarily cut him out of the our lives, we don't have to worry. As quickly as we say, "Lord Jesus Christ," he's back on the scene, ready to drag us out of the mud, wash off our filth, clothe us in holy garments, hug us, and send us on our way.

It is also true that we need to rest in Jesus' love. It's comforting to know that nothing is going to separate us "from the love of God that is revealed in Christ Jesus our Lord" (see Romans 8:38–39).

But maybe it's time to look at other aspects of Jesus. One way is to compare how Christians of former times viewed the Lord. For instance, early Christians used the term *Righteous One* to refer to Jesus. The title doesn't appear in the Gospels, although Pilate's wife urged her husband not to do anything to "that righteous man" in Matthew 27:19, although modern Bible versions tend to translate it as "innocent." At Jesus' death, the soldier declared, "He was certainly a righteous man" (Luke 23:47, NIV).

Righteous One as a title comes from Acts 3:14, 7:52, and 22:14. The early Church used the term for Jesus, probably getting their inspiration from Isaiah 53:11: "When he sees all that is accomplished by his anguish, he will be satisfied. And because of his experience, my righteous servant will make it possible for many to be counted righteous, for he will bear all their sins."

Eventually, the term passed out of use and never became a title for Jesus used by the Church in general. That's sad to me, because I like thinking of him as the Righteous One. It reminds us not only what Jesus *did*, but who he *is*.

Maybe it's time to emphasize righteousness today and to ask more about what those ancient believers meant. In the pre-Christian synagogues, godly people used *dikaois* (righteous) as the concept of the human ability to keep the law and to receive rewards. The righteous were those whose merits outweighed their faults.

Patriarchs, such as Abraham, head up the first level of the righteous, along with many outstanding teachers. They also taught that the prayers of the righteous turned God's thoughts from severity to mercy.

The young Church used *dikaois* to distinguish those who lived by being faithful to God's laws. So it was certainly appropriate to call Jesus the Righteous One. His nature and action conform to God's will. Paul even calls him *our* righteousness. In practical terms, when we see him as the Righteous One, then we who belong to him must also follow his example and do right (see 1 John 2:29). Then we are righteous.

That's where we draw back. How often do we pray, "Lord Jesus, make me righteous as you are righteous"? It's not that we want to do evil, but we don't feel comfortable praying about being righteous. Something about that word smacks of *self*-righteousness or hints of hypocrisy. It makes us sound like the Pharisees, the so-called pure ones of Jesus' day, who prided themselves on their scrupulous observance of the law.

That's exactly where we have trouble. We want to live in such a way that we don't break God's laws and that everything we do pleases God, but we hardly know how to pray to the Righteous One to be made righteous.

Sometimes I have prayed, "God, I want to be right with you." That's the kind of prayer that comes after I know I've done wrong and want to clear up the mess. Or I've felt a vague kind of estrangement. Or maybe it comes as a kind of renewing nudge from God.

For a few days I've been struggling with praying to the Righteous One to help me reflect *dikaois* in my daily living. Recently, I decided to say it plainly. "God, make me a righteous person." I didn't mean it in the ancient Jewish mode of having more good things to my credit than bad. I didn't mean some kind of accounting that enabled me to be declared not guilty in a legal sense.

"God, make me a righteous person." When I prayed those words, my mind moved toward the Righteous One, to my desire to be more like Jesus Christ. As I meditated, I sensed I had inched a little closer to the meaning of what I sought. Jesus is the one who is holy, the one who does only what is right, the one who judges each situation and person correctly, because Jesus knows the whole truth (and all the lies).

None of us will ever attain to that level of practical *dikaois* or ever be fully righteous, but we can lean on the Righteous One. As long as we continue to walk toward Jesus, we're becoming more like him.

In this connection, I thought of one of my favorite short stories, Nathaniel Hawthorne's "The

Great Stone Face." A man named Ernest stared at the shape of a face on a mountain's escarpment day after day, year after year. In time, his face took on the look of the great stone face. He *became* the great stone face.

That's what I want for me and for all believers—for us to be so linked to the Righteous One that each day we resemble him a little more. The transformation begins when we pray, "Make me righteous as you are righteous."

> But now you must be holy in everything you do, just as God who chose you is holy. For the Scriptures say, "You must be holy because I am holy" (1 Peter 1:15–16).

Oh, righteous One,
sometimes I feel unclean around you,
aware of my lack of perfection,
very much wanting to hide my nakedness.
Make me righteous,
as you are righteous. Amen.

Chapter Twenty-Two
The Faithful One

"Why do you tell me things I don't want to hear?" I asked David Morgan.

"Because I'm your friend," he said softly.

Then I hugged him. He had just said something to me that I didn't find easy to accept. I attempted humor as a response while I mentally pushed myself to accept his words.

That's one of the reason I love David: He's faithful. His actions make me think of Proverbs 27:6, "The kisses of an enemy may be profuse, but faithful are the wounds of a friend" (NIV).

That hasn't been the normal way I've thought of faithfulness, especially with God. When I've used the term, I've tended to think of the doggedness of God to stay true to the divine nature and to be there to urge us onward.

Here are two verses I memorized early in my Christian experience that helped me with that perception: "The temptations in your life are no different from what others experience. And God is faithful. He will not allow the temptation to be more than you can stand. When you are tempted, he will show you a way out so that you can endure" (1 Corinthians 10:13). The second verse, even though the word faithful isn't used in it, has the same idea: "And I am certain that God, who began the good work within you, will continue his work until it is finally finished on the day when Christ Jesus returns" (Philippians 1:6).

More recently, God's faithfulness has taken on a tone of compassion and warmth, of protection and guidance. It has become the "love that wilt not let me go." God's faithfulness has been epitomized for me by Lamentations 3:22–23: "The faithful love of the Lord never ends! His mercies never cease. Great is his faithfulness; his mercies begin afresh each morning."

When I talk to the Faithful One, I now think of the one who dares to speak the truth to me, the one who tells me both the good and the bad news about myself. But along with that is the underlying compassion that says, "I love you enough to tell you what you don't want to hear."

As an example of this, in John 4, Jesus goes to a well in Samaria, sits down by the well, and asks a woman to draw water and give him a drink. Being a Samaritan, she is hated by Jews, but she gives Jesus the water. In their conversation, he asks her to call her husband and she says she has none. Jesus then tells her she has had five husbands and is now living with a man to whom she isn't married. Although he speaks the truth, Jesus doesn't reproach or condemn her. He states the facts and she listens. After he talks to her about God, she runs back to her village. "Come and see a man who told me everything I ever did!" (John 4:29).

We don't know all the things Jesus said to her, but one thing we can be sure of: He made God's love a reality to her, or she wouldn't have run back to the village and spread the good news.

As in Jesus, when he talked to the woman, I perceive faithfulness in David Morgan, who sometimes tells me unpleasant things but in such a way that he makes me know he cares about me. Sometimes it hurts me to hear the truth, but the lovingly faithful don't back away.

Faithfulness also speaks to us of truth we haven't accepted or perceived. And it's not always bad. When I was a pastor in the 1980s, I often asked people to repeat after me when I closed the pastoral prayer: "Loving God, show me the truth about myself, no matter how beautiful it may be."

I stood at the pulpit, my eyes open, and watched. I loved to see the surprise on visitors' faces when they heard those words. Many times people said, "I expected to hear you say 'no matter how bad it may be.'"

Perhaps it's because many of us have come out of a religious climate of denunciation and we expect nothing else. It's certainly true of me. I did attend Sunday school and church as a child. But one day, when I was about ten years old, I sat in church while the pastor stormed at us for our terrible sins. I knew then I was going to hell.

Then why am I sitting here? I asked myself. If I'm going to hell anyway, this sure isn't any fun. More than a decade passed before I walked inside a church again.

Even when I came to God, those thoughts of damnation were still there. It took me a few years before I valued the faithfulness of God. As I have grown in my Christian experiences, I've sensed God's stinging rebuke, and it has hurt deeply, and yet I know it was divine faithfulness at work.

God wants all of us to walk along the golden brick road that leads ultimately to perfection. God knows—and so do we—that we're not going to reach the place called Perfect, but we keep going. God's compassionate faithfulness constantly encourages us.

Sometimes God's faithfulness leaves me feeling sad, momentarily depressed or angry at myself for being so stiff-necked. But another part of me rejoices. I think, *How good of God to tell me the very things I don't want to hear.* Out of a loving heart, God speaks the words I need to hear.

When we pray, we can invoke that faithfulness. "Show me the truth about myself, whatever it is," we can pray. God's eternal, compassionate vigilance assures that the Faithful One is always there to speak what we need to hear.

God will make this happen, for he who calls you is faithful (1 Thessalonians 5:24).

But the Lord is faithful; he will strengthen you and guard you from the evil one (2 Thessalonians 3:3).

Faithful One,
make me want to hear your words,
give me the grace to open my heart,
and, God, show me the truth about myself,
no matter how beautiful it may be. Amen.

Chapter Twenty-Three
The Special Guide

"He leadeth me, O blessed thought...." "Guide me, O Thou Great Jehovah...."

In the church, we sing a lot of hymns about guidance. If we listen carefully to the way we sing, this business of getting God's guidance is a snap for us.

The simple formula, based on the Bible, takes only three steps:

1. Perceive a need for guidance.
2. Confess any sin that hinders the relationship.
3. Ask God to guide you, enable you to believe, and you receive.

I love it when God whispers, "This is the way, take it," and then I go forward. However, there's one problem with the formula: It doesn't always work.

God guides us, but not like any guide I've ever known in my life. For instance, I've traveled several times to Europe with a group. In each country, and sometimes in each city, we have a tour guide who shows us the sights, explains the history and culture, and answers our questions. Those guides seem to know everything. Once in Munich, Germany, we had three days of activities planned and were falling behind. The guide decided not to take us to Dachau, one of Hitler's labor camps.

"That's one thing I don't want to miss," I said. "I'll drop out of something else, but I want to see Dachau."

She shrugged and said, "All right, we'll go to Dachau and cut out something else."

I like that kind of guidance: I know what I want, I ask for it, and I get it.

Then why doesn't God work on some simple, direct system like that? I don't know, but the more I ask for divine guidance, the more I realize it deviates from a simple mathematical law most of us learned before seventh grade: The shortest distance between two points is a straight line.

The law of math may be true, but God doesn't seem to work with straight lines when it comes to guidance. Through reflecting on my own experiences and those of other Christians, I've realized that the Lord actively leads us into side paths, detours, and circuitous trips. That is, God's will seldom seems to be a straight line from conversion to glory.

Think about a few biblical characters and their experiences with guidance. "I'm going to give you a son," God told Abraham, "and he will have so many descendants that it would be easier to count the grains of sand than to number them."

Abraham was childless and seventy-five years old when he heard the wonderful news. He waited, and I'm sure he must have bombarded heaven with prayers. God did give him a son—when old Abe was one hundred.

When the Israelites prepared to leave Egypt for the Promised Land, God didn't send them by the most direct way: "When Pharaoh finally let the people go, God did not lead them along the main road that runs through Philistine territory, even though that was the shortest route to the Promised Land.... So God led them in a roundabout way through the wilderness toward the Red Sea" (Exodus 13:17–18). In this case, the Bible gives the reason: God said, "If the people are faced with a battle, they might change their minds and return to Egypt" (v. 17).

What kind of guidance did God give poor Joseph by letting the brothers throw him into a pit? Was there guidance when he was sold into slavery? Or when he was unjustly imprisoned for two years?

Or take David's kingship. Samuel the prophet-priest secretly anointed David to be the next king because, "I have rejected Saul," God said. For the next thirty plus years, David ran from Saul's armies, fearing for his life. He lived in caves, hid in out-of-the-way cities, and still the king pursued him. Hmm, some guidance.

We can see this in the life of Jesus. He had been ministering around Jerusalem and then headed toward Cana of Galilee. John 4:4 reads, "He had to go through Samaria on the way."

He did? Jesus could have followed the seacoast road without going to Samaria. Or he could have taken one that wound through Perea. Either road would have been shorter and more commonly used by Jews of his day. But Jesus took the long way because he "had to go." The King James Version says, even more strongly, "must needs go through."

Of course, all that leads up to a delightful story of Jesus meeting a fallen woman of Samaria at the well, his telling her about God, and her apparent conversion and witnessing that brought the whole town to hear him.

How does this work for people like us today? Asking God to guide is a recurring topic for most of us, and I never seem to get it straight. Dozens of times I've laid out a perfectly logical plan that leads me from A to B to C to D, and I tell God. Often, my Special Guide ignores all my efforts and plans, and takes me another way. Sometimes I reach point D. Sometimes I end up at point K.

How does our Special Guide lead us then? First, our Special Guide knows what's ahead. Sometimes what we want to see or do may not be as simple as it looks to us. We don't know that we can't cross a gorge up ahead because there's no bridge and we have to detour four miles. Sometimes God, aware of the temptations ahead, takes us on a different path because we're not strong enough to win the battle.

Second, our Special Guide has different purposes than we do. Intellectually and theologically, we know we're microscopic dots on the face of this great world. But we get confused and try to make ourselves the center of the universe. Our Special

Guide doesn't indulge our fantasy, but takes us through humbling experiences to teach us reality. There are more needs to be met than our own.

Third, God never promised Abraham, Moses, Peter, or anyone else that guidance would function like a visit to a psychic. We don't go to God to get spiritual palm readings. We tend to think that if we conjure up plans and seek God's seal of approval (i.e., guidance), then *voila!* it comes to pass.

Is it possible we have it all wrong? Is it possible that we have no real sense of what's important for our good and our growth? Is it possible that God really knows the best plan for us and determines to fulfill it despite our resistance or arguments?

Maybe our Special Guide wants us to figure out that, through all those side roads, bypaths, and circuitous routes, God really has only a single purpose for us. That purpose is that we would " become like his Son " (see Romans 8:29). That's a theological way of saying God brings all these divergent forces into our lives to make us like Jesus.

We're all for the end product. Our problem is what it takes to get there.

When we talk, our Special Guide listens—maybe with a twinkle and a grin—especially when we've explained how to run the section of the universe that applies to us. Ever tactful and kind, the Special Guide whispers, "Be at peace. Everything is working together for your good and you're moving closer to my purpose in your life. I'm going to keep working with you so I can make you more and more like Jesus."

That tells me how to pray. We can ask our Special Guide to take us down the paths we need to follow so that when we get to the end of them, we'll "become like his Son."

> Your word is a lamp to guide my feet and a light for my path. LORD, accept my offering of praise, and teach me your regulations. My life constantly hangs in the balance, but I will not stop obeying your instructions (Psalm 119:105, 108–109).

> *Divine Guide,*
> *forgive me when I try to tell you*
> *how to direct me on my pathway.*
> *I stumble often because I get too far away*
> *from your light.*
> *Thanks for grabbing me by the shoulders, hugging me, and saying gently,*
> *"Here, this is the way. Walk in it."*
> *Thanks, Guide of my life. Amen.*

Chapter Twenty-Four
My Guiding Light

I decided to go for a walk through the wooded area of the retreat center in North Carolina. When I started, I reveled in the crescent moon and the few stars that barely broke through the darkness. I paused to watch clouds snake their way across the horizon. Each seemed darker than the one before it.

It was probably stupid to go for a walk at 10:30 at night in a place I'd never been before, even though they had marked the paths well. But I needed to get away from everyone else, to think, pray, and clear my head.

For several minutes, I walked with my mind unfocused. I listened to the discordant sounds of night creatures, breathed deeply, and felt the coolness of the air on my bare arms. Fireflies flickered as they danced before me, and the constant sound of the frogs kept their beat in the background.

Quite suddenly a cloud layer covered the nascent moon; every shadow dissipated into total darkness. I pulled the flashlight out of my pocket, tripped, dropped the flashlight and landed on my outstretched hands. When I picked myself up, thankful I had only minor scratches on my palms, I retried my flashlight, but it refused to work. Then it struck me: I'd have to walk the rest of the winding trail in inky blackness.

I moved cautiously forward, mostly by feeling the branches of the trees on either side of the path. No matter how straight I tried to walk, I constantly veered to the left. At one point, I laughed to myself as I envisioned myself down on hands and knees, crawling so I could feel the edge of the path.

I had stumbled around for perhaps ten minutes, when a bright beam broke through the darkness. Apparently, a car had driven up to the retreat house, and the driver forgot to turn off the lights. They made a perfect beacon for me to follow.

"What a difference a light makes," I said aloud as I rushed along the path.

In remembering that incident years later, it occurs to me that the darker the world, the more important it is for us to see a ray of light guiding us along the road. Once in a while, the path becomes so clear we couldn't miss it. More often, we get what would amount to about twelve inches of light on the path ahead. Those twelve inches are just enough to take one step forward.

It reminds me of the time the Israelites were about to enter the Promised Land after years of wandering in the wilderness. The priests, who led the vast procession, approached the Jordan when the river was at flood stage. "But as soon as the feet of the priests who were carrying the Ark touched the water at the river's edge, the water above that point began backing up a great distance away ..." (Joshua 3:15–16).

That's about the way the Guiding Light operates in our lives, no matter how fervently we pray for ten yards or five miles of insight. That bit of guidance is enough to start the decision-making process. But in our impatience, we want it all spelled out before we put our toes into the Jordan.

Sometimes I'm a bit envious of those people who always seem to see six miles ahead and get no surprises in life. No matter how much I pray for guiding light, I seldom see searchlight-strength beams. In fact, if anything, I seem to have less light ahead of me than I did when I was new in the faith.

As I wrote that last sentence, a beam of interior light flashed through my brain. The Christian life means walking by faith, not by sight. (See 2 Corinthians 5:7.) Is it possible that having less light on the path may be a way for us to realize that we've grown closer to God? For most of us, it's easier to trust God when everything goes well, when we know what we're doing and where we're going. But what about when we face blackouts, roadblocks, and detour signs?

"Maybe God trusts you enough to let you walk on without a lot of outward guidance," a friend once said when I complained. "Maybe that's divine approval."

Once in a while, there's no light. It's not total darkness, but it's more like a pre-dawn condition. I've been there a few times and so have most of us who seek God's light. No matter which way we look, our eyes see only grayness. "Do I go forward?" we ask. "Turn around? Go to the left?"

For eighteen months, beginning in 1995, I lived in a world of hazy gray, no matter how much light I sought. "What do I do now, Guiding Light?" I prayed one day. After a lengthy silence, I felt emotionally low. I had decisions to make and no sense of direction. I had been walking for months without any beam of light and needed something to guide me. "Just a glimmer, a tiny sliver of light, anything," I asked.

I got nothing except part of a verse I had learned many years ago: "I will never fail you. I will never abandon you" (Hebrews 13:5). That wasn't the word I *wanted* to hear, but it was the message I *needed* to hear.

The message slowly sank in. God was with me. That was all I needed to know right then.

Sometimes we have to go on without obvious light to guide us. Some days we pray, watching for the Guiding Light to shine, and none comes, so we have to move forward and trust God that we're choosing the right path.

That's scary for people like me. I'm one of those who wants God to direct every part of my life. And it's not easy for me to make my choices without a divine response.

When this happens, maybe it's God's way to say that we're enough in touch with the Guiding Light that we know without having to see the light. We pray for light and it may not always be obvious, but it's there.

Maybe it means the Guiding Light is shining brightly within and not on the pathway.

> Jesus spoke to the people once more and said, "I am the light of the world. If you follow me, you won't have to walk in the darkness, because you will have the light that leads to life" (John 8:12).

Guiding Light,
I commit myself to follow you—
even when the darkness increases—
because I know you're always with me.
I trust you not to let me walk in darkness. Amen.

Chapter Twenty-Five
The Good Shepherd

"I'm glad Jesus was a shepherd and not a rancher," one of my friends said. After we laughed, he explained. "Shepherds know the names of every sheep and every lamb. It's a very personal relationship. Shepherds live with their animals, and are there to protect them all the time. Ranchers, however, have such huge herds, the animals are essentially numbers to them."

I hadn't thought about that before, but as soon as I did, I felt overjoyed that Jesus called himself the Good Shepherd and not the Top Rancher. In one of his famous lessons, Jesus said, "I am the good shepherd; I know my own sheep, and they know me" (John 10:14).

As I typed that verse, I paused to give thanks to God for the connection: The Good Shepherd knows us, and we, the sheep, know our Shepherd. A few minutes ago, I reread verses at the end of John 10, verses from which I have often found comfort, one of which is: "My sheep listen to my voice; I know them, and they follow me" (10:27).

The trouble for me is that I don't always hear the Shepherd's voice. In fact, I get quite confused sometimes in listening for it.

I'm long past *not* listening; that is, I don't deliberately plug up my ears. But my self-deception may have taken over. That system functions best when I want something badly and ask the Good Shepherd, "Please, may I have it?"

Sometimes I get a faint yes, but often it's the voice of inner desire rather than the Shepherd giving permission.

I don't have a monopoly on self-deception. Haven't all of us heard others say, "The Lord told me ..."? Or "The Lord showed me ..."?

Several editors have told me stories about getting manuscripts from sincere people who say, "God told me to write this and that you would publish it." More than one editor has told me, "We've never found one of those 'inspired' manuscripts worth publishing."

I remember an evangelist who tried to raise money in a worship service by saying, "God told me that five people would give a thousand dollars tonight. Quickly, who are you?" Only one person responded.

The speaker played that note for a while and then he said, "How many of you will give a hundred? We'll get our five thousand that way."

He didn't realize what he had said, and he may have been a fraud. But I don't think most people are intentionally lying when they say God told them something that doesn't work out. I want to make it clear that I believe the Good Shepherd speaks to us, his sheep. The Bible says so, and I've heard the voice myself.

"Why is it," my wife once asked the Good Shepherd, "that I don't always know when it's your voice?"

She received an answer. She never claimed it was from God, but it sounded pretty good to me. "My *sheep* hear my voice; my *lambs* are still learning."

I don't like being called a lamb. It sounds so immature. But I act like a lamb at times, and the Shepherd, who knows my name, understands. As I pray to the Good Shepherd, I envision myself as a tiny lamb like I've seen in depictions of Jesus the Good Shepherd. Then I feel warm, loved, and protected.

Of course, there's also a picture of Jesus the Good Shepherd leaning down the side of a cliff to save one stupid lamb that ran away. It hadn't listened to the shepherd's voice or it wouldn't have tumbled over.

Yes, I can see myself as that little lamb, cowering, frightened, and waiting. Even though I know the Good Shepherd is reaching for me, I still get scared, and I feel ashamed. I think of the verse that says, "All of us, like sheep, have strayed away. We have left God's paths to follow our own ..." (Isaiah 53:6).

Just because we all go astray doesn't excuse us. It means we have to *learn* to listen. We have to examine our hearts. And even when we have an answer, sometimes we need to wait, to keep asking until we're positive it's the Good Shepherd speaking and not our self-deception at work.

I've been praying to hear the voice of the Good Shepherd, to hear it so distinctly and clearly I won't miss it. This reminds me of the voice of the singer B. J. Thomas. When I turn on the radio and hear him singing, I smile, especially when it's one of his songs that I like. Sometimes, however, I hear other singers that sound like him with that country-and-western style, and I get confused. Yet when B. J. sings, I don't ever think he's somebody else. I know his voice when I hear it.

Isn't that the way it is for many of us? Sometimes we hear a voice that sounds a little like the Good Shepherd, but we're not sure. That's when we get into trouble. We want so badly to hear the Shepherd's voice that we act when it's one that sounds only "a little" like his. Yet in those moments when the Good Shepherd speaks to us through that quiet, loving voice, we recognize the sound that's not like any other voice. Then we know the Good Shepherd is leading us.

> My sheep listen to my voice; I know them, and they follow me. I give them eternal life, and they will never perish. No one can snatch them away from me (John 10:27–28).

Good Shepherd,
thank you for your infinite patience.
I want to hear you.
I listen for your voice.
Sometimes I strain to hear you speak.
Is it because I want to hear you so badly
that I allow other voices to confuse me?
Help me, Good Shepherd, so that I'm tuned in to just your voice
and I won't listen to any other. Amen.

Chapter Twenty-Six
The Door

Jesus, a door? That's what he says about himself in John, chapter ten. For me at least, that was one of the strangest images of the Lord in the New Testament. Only after a bit of research did I figure out what it meant.

"Most assuredly, I say to you, he who does not enter the sheepfold by the door, but climbs up some other way, the same is a thief and a robber. But he who enters by the door, is the shepherd of the sheep. To him the doorkeeper opens ..." (vv. 1–3, NKJV).

In first-century villages, the people had communal sheepfolds to keep the animals in at night. The doorkeeper locked them inside and kept the key. During the warm weather, the sheep lived out on the hills. The shepherd didn't bring them back to the village at night, but stayed in the hillside sheepfolds—roofless buildings with an open space for a door. At night he curled up in his cloak and lay across the opening. No person or animal got in or out without the shepherd's knowledge.

Jesus said, "Most assuredly, I say to you, I am the door of the sheep ... I am the door. If anyone enters by Me, he will be saved, and will go in and out, and find pasture" (John 10:7, 9, NKJV).

Jesus used an illustration his hearers could easily grasp when he said that he was the door—the means of access to God (see Hebrews 10:20). Another way to say this is that Jesus opened a door where there had been no door. Until he came, there was no access to God. He is the living access and through him we enter into God's presence.

As I prayed about Jesus, the Door, I also thought of his words, "If anyone enters by me, he will be saved, and will go in and out and find pasture" (John 10: 9 NLJV).

A Jewish-Christian friend told me that "to go in and out" was a Hebraic expression. It was a statement of safety. It meant to be unharmed and secure. That's part of the promise God constantly gives us.

Jesus, the Door, encloses, but also shuts out. Recently, I've thought about the things in my life that the Divine Door has shut out. I have no intention of cataloging my sins BC (Before Christ). After all, God has already forgotten them. But more than specific acts I had committed, Jesus closed a number of doors in my life. It wasn't that he led me into a restrictive life, although some of my friends may have thought so. Some things were no longer appropriate for me as a Christian, and I turned my back on them.

For instance, when I became a Christian, I had already been a smoker for five or six years. I joined a group of people my age for a weekly Bible study, and I often pulled out a cigarette and lit up. To their credit, not one person ever condemned me or made me feel uncomfortable, although I was the only smoker.

One day, someone in the group talked about our bodies as temples of the Holy Spirit. He was talking about himself and how often he had defiled his body. I held a lighted cigarette in my hand at the time (but I didn't feel he aimed his comments at me). As I took another puff, those words hit me. I was defiling my body.

I decided to quit. It took a couple of weeks, but I kicked the habit and left cigarettes for good. This was long before anyone talked about the addictiveness of smoking. I quit because Jesus Christ closed a door for me.

God also closed relationship doors for me. I had dated a genuinely nice woman and had talked about marriage. But I sensed that if I married her, she would make it difficult, if not impossible, for me to follow God with all my heart. I agonized over the matter and finally broke off the relationship. Another door closed behind me.

For the first few months of my new-found faith, one "Jesus Door" after another was closed. Each time, I rejoiced, even though it was painful or difficult. I rejoiced because I felt I was doing the right thing.

Jesus Christ opened many doors in my life too. From my early teen years, I wanted to teach. When the door of faith opened, I felt I had values to impart, along with curriculum and content.

Doors of understanding opened as I learned to accept people who were different from me, some of whom have been friends for thirty years. Their open doors to me enriched my life.

In the same passage where Jesus called himself the door, he also promised, "I have come that they may have life, and that they may have it more abundantly" (10:10 NKJV). That's what the Divine Door represents most of all—abundant life. For me that doesn't mean wealth, prestige, power, or fame. Abundant life implies contentment, peace, a sense of being loved and belonging. It means the presence and good pleasure of God directed at me.

Jesus is the door that "hold up the shield of faith to stop the fiery arrows of the devil" (Ephesians 6:16, NLT). Yes, Jesus is my Door—the entrance of safety and assurance—that opens the way to God.

> I am the door. If anyone enters by Me, he will be saved, and will go in and out and find pasture.... I have come that they may have life, and that they may have it more abundantly (John 10:7–9 NKJV).

Cecil Murphey

⚜ ⚜ ⚜

Divine Door,
you are the entrance into a life of joy, peace and holiness,
and you are also the door that shuts evil
and darkness out of my life.
Thank you for being the entrance to all things
bright and beautiful in my life. Amen.

Chapter Twenty-Seven
The Divine Bread

Two days ago, I read in John's Gospel the Bible verses that contain the famous "I am the Bread of Life" passage.

The story begins in chapter six with the feeding of more than five thousand people. When a boy offers his lunch of a couple of tiny fish and five pieces of bread, Jesus miraculously feeds all the people and the disciples pick up twelve baskets of leftovers.

The people stay there that night, but Jesus goes to the other side of the lake. When the crowd figures it out, they find him. Jesus then says to them, "You want to be with me because I fed you, not because you understood the miraculous signs. But don't be so concerned about perishable things like food. Spend your energy seeking the eternal life that the Son of Man can give you" (John 6:26b–27).

Jesus compares himself to the manna God sent to the Israelites in the wilderness and declares himself the True Bread who came from heaven to give life to the world.

Although Jesus speaks in symbolic language, the crowd grasps what he means. He goes on to say that not only is he the Bread of Life, but whoever follows him won't hunger again and those who believe won't thirst.

At those words, some of them are offended. "Isn't he Joseph's son?" they ask each other. The more Jesus speaks, the more difficulty they have listening. They plead the inability to understand, but I think it's clear that they don't grasp what they don't want to know.

By the time Jesus finishes his message, most of the people have gone. He then turns to his disciples. "You do not want to leave too, do you?"

Simon Peter replied, "Lord, to whom would we go? You have the words that give eternal life. We believe, and know you are the Holy One of God" (John 6:68–69).

After reading the story, I felt fairly superior. I wasn't the crowd; I was Simon Peter. I have believed and followed.

Then my smugness vanished. Yes, I was following Jesus. But why? Was I as guilty of following for bread as the crowd? If Jesus tossed out bread or whatever else I needed and all I had to do in return was to follow, I'd probably squeeze toward the front of the line.

I don't like to admit it, but sometimes my question really is: What's in it for me? Or to put it differently, "What do I get out of following Jesus?"

Jesus would plead with us not to work for food that perishes, and urge listeners to work for what gives eternal life (and that could include eternal rewards). Hundreds of years earlier, Isaiah the prophet writes, "Why spend money on food that does not give you strength? Why pay for food that does you no good?" (Isaiah 55:2).

Both Isaiah and Jesus point to two kinds of hunger. We all have the physical kind—a gnawing inside that says, "It's time to eat." Under normal circumstances, we satisfy that hunger.

Both men also refer to something more important: spiritual hunger. I think they mean an unsatisfied longing, a yearning for something more than what we have, an experience that goes beyond our present level of relationship with God.

When Jesus fed the multitude, he satisfied the first kind. They followed him to get more free meals. He didn't deny them food, but he pushed them to accept the real message, that he was Divine Bread—ready to satisfy spiritual hunger. The crowd didn't want that.

But I do. I'm a Christian because one day I realized it was the Divine Bread I hungered for. I had tried a lot of different pleasures around me. They weren't always bad, were seldom boring, but they didn't last.

I remember when that became obvious to me. I was twenty years old and attended an office party. We told jokes, passed around the booze, and had a really fun time. I was in the middle of it.

Later I observed the others, thinking, *It's going to be over in a couple of hours. What then?* Some will be so hung over they won't get much work done tomorrow. All day long, we'll hear comments and jokes about the fun we had the night before. But it'll be hollow laughter.

I wish I could have said then, "Lord, give me the Divine Bread," but I didn't know those words. I wasn't aware that my inner hunger was for God.

Now years later, I realize that, like the crowd that followed Jesus, I've been willing to settle for things that only temporarily satisfy my appetite, and I've been concerned too little about hungering for more of the Divine Bread.

I wonder if spiritual hunger is something we can want, pray for, and then it happens. Or does God put the desire in us to want it and then we pray for it?

At times, when I've talked to God, it's been like eating three-day-old toast. Every bit demanded a lot of work and total commitment. On other days, I've felt such a yearning for more of God; when I prayed, I felt the Lord's closeness.

So first, I've asked God to make me hunger—every day of my life—for more of the Holy Bread of Life.

I've also asked, "God, once you begin to satisfy my spiritual hunger, how do I keep it going? How do I keep yearning for more of the Divine Bread?"

I received no answer, but in the silence I reflected on how to be more sensitive to spiritual hunger. Jesus pronounced those who hunger and thirst after righteousness as blessed or happy. That's what I yearn for—that ongoing relationship of blessedness. Great Christian writers of the past say that God alone can truly satisfy the hunger of the soul he himself created and into which he put the hunger for himself.

I'm sure they're right, but that still leaves me asking, "How? How do I keep hungering? How can I keep yearning for God?"

Like everything else in life, my yearning for Divine Bread fluctuates. Some days I yearn for God more deeply than on others. When I go through the low periods, when God seems a little less energizing in my life, I'm learning to accept that God is there. I may not feel a holy presence or have any strong sense of guidance, but God is still there.

This also reminds me that we never cross that line between the human and divine. I'm always going to be imperfect in my perceptions and flawed in my desires. That's what being a sinful human being means.

Today as I finished praying, I thought, *God, it's so exciting that I hunger for you today. I'm thankful that I feel a dissatisfied yearning for a closer walk with you. Help me make the most of it while it's here.*

Just then I thought of Peter's sermon on the Day of Pentecost when he referred to times of refreshing from the presence of the Lord (see Acts 3:19 NIV). That means not all the time and not even every day, but at times God refreshes us.

For the past couple of months, I've been stirring myself in my spiritual discipline. My task is to open myself as much as I know how. I can fill myself with Bible reading, worshiping with other Christians, and partaking of the Lord's Table.

> As the deer longs for streams of water, so I long for you, O God. I thirst for God, the living God (Psalm 42:1–2).
>
> Taste and see that the Lord is good (Psalm 34:8).

Divine Bread,
cause me to hunger for you today.
Enable me to yearn for more of your life in me.
On those days when I feel stuffed and satisfied with myself,
surprise me, and stir me up with a
renewed hunger. Amen.

Chapter Twenty-Eight
The Pioneer of Our Faith

When I lived in Kenya, East Africa, I agreed to take two American guests into Masai territory early one Sunday morning. The Masai tribe, much photographed and studied, were nomadic and the last resisters of westernization in that part of the country.

Sangra, who spoke Masai, guided the three of us. We drove my Volkswagen Bug until the dirt road ended. "How far is it now?" asked Jim, one of the Americans.

"Not far. Perhaps one mile," Sangra said. He pointed to the top of a high hill. "Just over there." (The day before, he told me that he hadn't been there before, but he could find it without any trouble. I had been with him on enough treks that I trusted him implicitly to get us there.)

From Sangra's answer, I knew it could be one mile or four miles. I also knew that "just over there" could easily mean over there, down the hill and up another. I wasn't totally wrong. We went up three hills, each higher than the previous.

"Where's the trail? Which way?" asked Jack, the other American, as we started our upward climb.

Despite the lack of any obvious trail, Sangra kept going forward and we followed behind him single file. The unmatted grass had grown perhaps two feet high at the place we started. Obviously, no one had been up that way for a long, long time.

"Are you sure he knows where he's going?" Jack whispered to me more than once.

"Why would he lead us astray?" I said.

"You think maybe he's lost?"

"I don't think so. He knows the area."

Our "perhaps one mile" kept us walking for more than two hours. My two friends, unused to such strenuous effort and still new to the tropics, were exhausted when we reached the clearing just before high noon. Nearly fifty Masai sat and waited for us. After a service that lasted well over two hours, we started back.

"He's not going the right way," Jack kept saying. "He's taking a different route." He pointed to the direction we had traversed before.

"We'll get there," I kept saying. I was tired from the walk, and I had preached more than an hour, standing in the hot sun. My guests' fears wore on my nerves. Finally, I just ignored them.

We made the trip back in less time than it had taken us to go.

That incident illustrates what it means to follow Jesus, the "pioneer and perfecter of our faith." Scholars have translated it several ways, including *author and finisher*, but I like the concept of pioneer. When I call Jesus by that term, I think of him as the ground breaker, the one who goes ahead of us into the unknown. He blazes the trail for us.

Sangra wasn't Jesus, but he certainly exemplified the pioneer quality. He never hesitated, never backtracked, and never looked around to get his bearings. He knew where he was going, understood we depended on him to lead us, and he got all three of us there.

The difference between my two friends and me is that I was used to Sangra. He had led me before. I trusted him, and I never had any doubts. Jim and Jack, however, knew nothing about Africa, other than viewing Tarzan movies and reading a couple of glowing missionary reports. They had come to Africa about as ignorant as any visitors I'd ever seen. They fretted and complained of the heat. They wanted to stop every twenty minutes and rest.

Most of us are like Jack and Jim in our journey through life. We don't know what's ahead and could easily get lost. It's important to trust the Pioneer and follow, despite our doubts.

I can sum up the kind of travel I envision as I pray to the Pioneer of My Faith by referring to a chorus we used to sing years ago called, "Where He Leads Me, I Will Follow." He's constantly taking me into new territory—new for me—but since his lonely trek to Calvary, he has known the way. Jesus himself said, "I am the way...." Hebrews 10:20 says that by his death he made a "new and life-giving way."

The problem is, *I* don't know the way. That uncertainty makes it a fearful journey at times. Like Jack, I keep thinking, wondering, worrying, and trying to give directions.

As we approached the second hill on that trip, Jack had pointed to a more gradual slope we could climb, but Sangra shook his head. He didn't stop to explain. On the way back to the car, we understood. The gentle slope hid a deep, rocky ravine.

The guide who's been there before knows the way. As I meditate on that concept, it makes me realize the futility of my worries and concerns.

Sometimes I feel like turning back, but I don't want to be like the unbelieving Israelites in the wilderness, who cried out, "Have you brought us out here to die?" Despite divine assurances, promises, and daily provisions for their needs, they wanted to go back to Egypt. Every new experience brought trembling and grumbling.

I see places ahead that scare me too and make me wonder if I'm going to make it. I even hear myself asking, "How long, God? How far (or how long) until you answer my prayer? How far do I have to go before you free me from this temper? How far is it before you fix it so that I don't worry about my children? About money? About relationships?"

Just like Sangra, Jesus doesn't usually answer directly. He simply points always ahead, showing me the right direction. He encourages me to keep on walking. It's as though he whispers, "I know you're tired, but you can make it. Just keep following me. You can do it."

And I know I will.

As I think about the completed journey, I recall when Sangra finally led us to the summit of the final hill. While we were surging upward, we didn't notice much of the landscape. We just wanted to get there. But once we reached the top, Jack paused, turned around, and looked back. He couldn't see the car or the dirt road we had followed, but he could see that we had come a long way. "Hey, we made it," he said as he wiped perspiration from his face.

Yes, we had made it. Time after time, we take the little journeys in life, going through new or strange territory. We're often unsure of where we're going. And perhaps it's only after we get there, when we can pause, turn around and look back, that we can reflect on what's happened.

"We did it. We made it."

Those are the words the Pioneer of our Faith wants to hear. Perhaps even more, he would love to hear us say as we trek upward, "We're going to make it. It's just a little farther."

> Therefore, since we are surrounded
> by such a huge crowd of witnesses to
> the life of faith, let us strip off every

weight that slows us down, especially the sin that so easily trips us up. And let us run with endurance the race God has set before us. We do this by keeping our eyes on Jesus, the champion who initiates and perfects our faith. Because of the joy awaiting him, he endured the cross, disregarding its shame. Now he is seated in the place of honor beside God's throne (Hebrews 12:1–2).

Pioneer of Our Faith,
I'm grateful that you've been there before,
and you know everything that lies ahead.
Forgive me when I fret or complain,
and remind me that you're always there to lead me. Amen.

Chapter Twenty-Nine
The Victor Over Temptation

I don't think I've ever wanted to murder anyone. I've never worshiped an idol. Adultery hasn't been a stumbling block for me. Why would I want to steal from someone? Such big sins don't bother me.

Most of us who seek to follow the leadership of Jesus Christ discover that the big lures tend to disappear. It's the little traps that we stumble into.

One of my little struggles is that I tend to ignore the warning signs of past experiences, cautions in the Bible, or the restraining hand of God. I'm amazed (in retrospect) how easily I convince myself to say a certain thing or act a certain way as a means of standing up for myself or being honest, or being faithful to point out another's shortcomings. Once in a while, I've quoted Bible verses to show my righteousness and purity of heart.

And yet ... I still give in to temptations.

No one has to tell me that I sin with my tongue. It's too quick to speak, and too slow to pause. Then why haven't I corrected it?

First, of course, is the old standby excuse of innate sin. I'm a sinner by nature, and I'll always be a sinner. I may get better, and by God's grace, I'll grow, but committing sin will always be part of me. Although true, it's no excuse for irresponsibility.

A far stronger reason is that I get confused between what I need and what I think I need. For instance, when King Ahab wanted to buy a certain vineyard and the owner refused to sell, he fell into deep depression. As king he probably had hundreds of vineyards, but he had to have that particular one. Its importance grew until he convinced himself he couldn't be happy without owning that piece of land.

"Hey, man, you're the king," his wife told him. "You can do what you want." She arranged for a couple of thugs to accuse the owner of a crime, she had him stoned, and the crown took over the property.

What about David and his sin with Bathsheba? If any man in the Bible knew the way of God, it was David, but even he allowed his desires to do his thinking for him. He may have had some unmet needs. Probably all of us think we do. Those are the things that get us into trouble, and sometimes we surrender to temptation. Yet as the Victor Over Temptation shows us our particular areas of weakness, we can resist the subtle lures around us.

As I have discussed this matter with the Victor, he has given me some insight about myself. It's more truthful to say, he's forced me to admit things about myself in recent days. Here's what I've learned. I know I'm a helper. People depend on me, talk to me, and open up to me. Sounds good and noble, doesn't it?

The Victor Over Temptation has been enabling me to see my underside, and I've finally begun to admit I feel pride in being needed and being indispensable. To please others, I've adapted to their demands and wishes. Especially in the past, I found it difficult to recognize my own lack because I spent so much energy in being needed. Unconsciously, I change my perspective to become empathetic and make emotional connections. Sometimes I adapt to the wishes of others as a way to gain or retain their love.

Until a few months ago, I lived in ignorance of those facts. As I continue to ask the Victor Over Temptation for help, however, I see myself more clearly. With God's help, I can find freedom from such traps.

The more I know about myself, and the more I'm in touch with the Victor, the more assured I become that I have the best weapons for defense. Those weapons are simple, yet they're effective only when we learn to use them.

First, I pray. More and more, I realize the importance of the words: "And don't let us yield to temptation, but rescue us from the evil one" (Matthew 6:13). I keep that petition before me because I want

God to show me the areas where I'm susceptible. As the Victor Over Temptation shows me my inner self, I often resist the truth. Yet as I ask him to enable me to be open and I listen, I also fortify myself to win the next battle.

Second, I'm reading more in my Bible. That's the most powerful way God speaks to me. I'll read along and a verse takes on power as if I'd never read it before.

Here's one example. I was involved in a controversy in a writers organization. One day when I was reading in Romans, my eyes stopped at this verse: "Do all that you can to live in peace with everyone" (12:18). The verse shouted inside my head. I read it two or three times. By then, I knew I had to do something to bring peace. I reexamined my position and realized my hidden needs had subverted my zeal for integrity. Once I backed up two steps, those on the other side did the same. We came to a place of peace.

That's the practical working of the Victor Over Temptation in my life. He helps me see not just the wrong and stupid things I've done; he's also helping me look below my actions and attitudes to figure out why I failed.

As I thought of this, I recalled a prominent pastor involved in an adulterous situation. He had sinned. At the same time, as I understand my proclivity to temptation, I'm learning to understand others. I wondered what kind of unfulfilled needs he had. If he had been able to talk to the Victor about those deep inner needs, he might have overcome the temptation.

No single temptation strikes all of us. As we open ourselves to the Victor Over Temptation, we can begin to understand our own inner driving forces that might ensnare us. Then comes victory.

As I become aware of my personal temptations, and as I call on the Victor Over Temptation, I know that I'm going to sin.

> If you think you are standing strong, be careful not to fall. The temptations in your life are no different from what others experience. And God is faithful. He will not allow the temptation to be more than you can stand. When you are tempted, he will show you a way out so that you can endure (1 Corinthians 10:12–13).

Victor Over Temptation,
with your help I can win.
With your help
I can find answers and satisfy those hurting,
needy parts of my life.
With your help
I can win time after time against temptations.
Thanks for providing a way out. Amen.

Chapter Thirty
The Truth

"My name is Cec, and I'm a liar." That's how it would sound if I started something called Liars Anonymous (LA). The customary greeting of those in twelve-step programs seems to be saying, "That's how I used to be. The tendency is still there, but I don't do it anymore."

I wish I could join LA.

I can't because I'm still a practicing liar. Not that I go around telling the unbelievable tales that everyone snickers at and says, "Oh, yeah, right." Frankly, I'm a bit more subtle about my lying.

Like the prophet Isaiah, I am a man of unclean lips and I live in a land of unclean people. I live in a world where it's all right to lie if you don't get caught.

A few months ago, I watched part of a 1940 Bob Hope film called *Nothing but the Truth*. Hope played an inveterate liar who made a bet he could tell the truth for twenty-four hours. He won the bet—barely.

I'm not sure I'd win. I'm not sure many of us would, because we've learned to lie in hundreds of ways and those habits are part of our lives. Sometimes it's as simple as exaggeration. How many people have we heard who had surgery for gallstones and reported the surgeon said, "It's the largest gallstone I've ever seen." Somebody lied, unless the stones get bigger every operation.

I read recently that American men often report their height as one or two inches taller than they actually are. Celebrities such as Tom Cruise and Sylvester Stallone are officially listed as six feet tall, but people who have seen them say they don't quite measure up. I've heard that most women over thirty-five tend to subtract a couple of years off their age to appear younger. And overweight people tend to subtract ten pounds when they confess their weight.

Or we lie because we don't want to hurt someone's feelings. I recall once when a wanna-be writer came to our editing group, presented an article, and we edited it. I thought it was one of the worst pieces of writing I'd seen in years, but I couldn't say that. "You need a lot of work," I said. That was true, uh, well, as far as it went.

Or we lie to save face. Or maybe it becomes an unconscious matter of feeling a little more important than we really are. Or we lie by not speaking up to defend what we believe in.

What a contrast to the words of Jesus. "I am the way, the truth, and the life" (John 14:6). Jesus didn't merely speak the truth, he embodied truth. Any human can teach the truth; only Jesus lived it.

Perhaps this sounds like a small thing to get excited about. We don't go out and deliberately decide to lie. It just slips up on us, usually to make us look better in some way.

Yet Jesus wouldn't lie for any reason. He might wisely choose to remain silent, but he had nothing to hide and nothing to protect. Maybe that's the big difference: We still have things to protect. We don't like revealing our vastly imperfect selves, so we lie to ourselves (and to others who'll listen).

Yet I want to reflect Jesus the Truth in my daily life. It's not easy for me. And I'm not sure how far to carry it. Suppose I walk by Dick's house. He's my neighbor and a nice man. If he's outside, I often pause to chat. "How are you?" is invariably his first question.

"Fine," I say without variation.

Aside from the custom of giving that answer, what if the truth is it's been one exceptionally bad day, and my emotions flow four feet below sea level? Do I openly say, "Lousy"?

Or worse, when sales people call, they first ask the question, "How are you today, Mr. Murphey?" and don't say anything more until I reply, "Fine," or something else as meaningless.

Do I start telling them the truth about my physical, emotional, and spiritual condition? Probably not, and I wouldn't want to say, "You're not really interested, so tell me why you called." It might be a truthful answer, but not very kind.

Okay, so lying is part of our culture. And once we learn to lie in small ways, we soon become proficient at non-truth telling. I don't like it, and I don't want to accept it as a permanent factor in my life.

In recent weeks, I've cried out, "Make me a truth seeker." Sometimes I put it this way: "Help me to put away lying, which includes exaggeration."

This is a topic God and I discuss a lot. Mostly, I cry out for help and God listens. My desire is that it can be said of me, "Every word Cec speaks is true." Will I ever attain that? If Liars Anonymous will accept me, with the help of God and others who face the same problem, perhaps I can begin to celebrate months, even years, of verbal veracity.

While I struggled with this issue, I had one of those delightful moments of insight. Another neighbor, Frank, commented on his yard. "My goal isn't to have a perfect yard this year," he said. "My goal is to make it a little better every year."

That's it! I thought. Lying by silence, by exaggeration, by shading the truth, and all of the other forms—I can't destroy them with a single blow. But I can work on them.

I think I could stand up in LA and say, "I'm Cec, and I'm a liar, but the Truth is with me. Together we're making progress. I value truth-telling and rejoice in winning over temptation. I'm not perfect this year, but with the God of Truth helping me, I'm making progress."

Show me the right path, O Lord, point out the road for me to follow. Lead me by your truth and teach me, for you are the God who saves me. All day long I put my hope in you (Psalm 25:4–5).

Teach me your ways, O Lord, that I may live according to your truth (Psalm 86:11)!

I have lived according to your truth (Psalm 26:3).

God of All Truth,
put within me a desire for truth, honesty, and integrity.
Guard my lips from speaking deceitfully
or doing anything that negatively reflects on you. Amen.

Chapter Thirty-One
The Forgiving God

I had sinned. It was just that simple, except it was different this time. This time I *knew* my sinfulness, and I couldn't handle it. I had been a Christian for a decade, been trained for and ordained to the ministry. In fact, I was in East Africa as a missionary when the enormity of my sin hit me.

When I relate the facts, they don't sound like a big deal. One day in casual conversation with an African leader, I mentioned something—a true fact—about Eve, another missionary. With no intention of spreading gossip, he told two other people. The information then took wings and flew everywhere.

When Eve learned that the story had spread—even though true—and that it had started with me, she was furious.

"I'm sorry," I said. "I didn't know—"

"That's no excuse!"

She fired every verbal barrage at me she possessed. Her remarks devastated me, and I didn't try to defend myself. After she left, I went into my bedroom and dropped on my knees. "I'm sorry, God," I said. "I didn't mean to hurt her."

Instead of finding relief and feeling forgiven, the pain increased. I had sinned by gossiping. I knew enough theology to acknowledge that God had forgiven me, but emotionally, I sank deeper and deeper into despair.

I was a sinner.

I had failed God.

I had failed Eve.

Hundreds of other instances filled my thoughts—unkind words, careless actions, insensitive behavior, and even a few times when I had deliberately done something to get back at another person.

I defended myself to God. First, I had assumed most people knew about Eve's past. Second, she was a woman who had a remarkably warm relationship with gossip.

Despite my defenses, no relief came.

I knew the situation with Eve had only opened a sealed compartment of my life. The anguish of soul had little to do with Eve. I became aware of my innate sinfulness.

I had sinned against God many times. Who hadn't? Each time I confessed, God forgave me. That was how the Christian faith worked. Except this time it didn't seem so easy. I felt no forgiveness, no release from my failures and shortcomings. The more I prayed, the worse I felt.

"Is there no forgiveness for me?" I cried. "Is my sin so awful that I can't receive absolution?" My theological training died inside that room, and I didn't know if I could ever resuscitate it. I didn't care about what the Church taught or the facts of the faith.

I canceled my activities, returned to my bedroom, and prayed through the morning. By noon, I didn't want to eat or talk or even look at anyone. I felt as if the word *sinner* had been painted across my face.

I was a sinner.

I stayed in my room most of the afternoon. At first, my wife Shirley tried to comfort me, but she's a smart person and sensed that I had a spiritual battle going on inside. She left me alone.

For three days, I battled my sin. I must have read Psalm 51 a dozen times. That psalm is David's cry for forgiveness after he had committed adultery with Bathsheba and had her husband killed in battle. I particularly thought of his wail, "Against you, you only have I sinned."

I understood, and those words echoed from my own lips. I had hurt Eve. I had hurt hundreds of people, but right then I couldn't think about them. God was the one who mattered. I prayed and prayed, but no peace came.

By the third day, I realized something about myself. I wasn't a man who sinned. I was a sinner who lived out his natural bent. Everyone from Paul, through the early church fathers, to Augustine, to

Luther and Calvin had been saying that. But now I heard it.

I felt even more ashamed.

Sin moved from a concept to a personal reality. Until then, I would never have denied I was a sinner or that I failed God regularly. But over that three-day period, the reality of human sinfulness, and specifically, *my* sinfulness took on substance.

"God, help me. If you leave me to myself, I'll just keep on doing things like this. I won't get any better. I'll just repeat my sin in different forms."

Just before noon on the third day, the release came through a quiet inner assurance that God had forgiven me. Or perhaps better, I could finally accept forgiveness. Now I had peace. I relaxed and slept for several hours.

That experience made me conscious of the Forgiving God, the one who bathes us with love and makes us brightly clean. Even though I deserved nothing but punishment, inside my head I heard something like this from 1 John 2:1: "My dear children, I am writing this to you so that you will not sin. *But* [italics mine] if anyone does sin, we have an advocate who pleads our case before the Father. He is Jesus Christ, the one who is truly righteous."

I'm weak and yield to temptation. But through that experience, God became the Forgiver—a wonderful liberating reality—in my life. When I ignorantly or foolishly do wrong, God is there to forgive me. Even with that glorious understanding, I still have had to learn to forgive myself. How could I let go of my sin? Of my pain? Of my grief? I knew the standard (and true) answers:

"Just surrender it to God."

"Yield it to God."

"Commit yourself to God."

"Let go and let God."

I'd heard those zillions of times, but they left me with a problem. *How?* I knew *what* to do, but I didn't know *how*.

By contrast, some people don't seem to take their sinfulness seriously enough. For them, confession is like putting a coin into a newspaper kiosk—in goes the coin, out comes the newspaper. Just a simple transaction. It didn't work that mechanically for me. I agonized. Several of my friends said, "You're just too hard on yourself."

"Of course I am," I said, "but I don't know how to do differently."

Then they sent me another truckload of advice—true and all meaningful, but not helpful.

I wish I could end this chapter by saying that now I go into my private place of confession and say, "Father, forgive me, for I have sinned," and walk away at peace. But the fact is, the longer I'm a Christian, the more I struggle when I speak with the Forgiving God. "How can you keep forgiving me?" I ask. "Look at all the years I've been a Christian, and I know better."

At my best moments, I hear a voice inside that says, "I am on your side. Go, child, and sin no more."

Another plus for me is that in some churches they have a ritual for confession as part of their worship. Either they have specific prayers the people read together or the minister prays a prayer of confession. It touches me that at the end of the prayer, the minister says, "I declare to you in the name of Jesus Christ, we are forgiven."

The pastor doesn't forgive but declares or announces the good news of our forgiveness. That comforts me. Maybe because I hear a human voice telling me biblical truth. Maybe it makes me listen objectively instead of focusing subjectively on my sinful state. Whatever the reason, when I hear those words, most of the time, I am able to take a deep breath and whisper to myself, "Cec, I declare to you in the name of Jesus Christ, you are forgiven."

And I know I am.

> Have mercy on me, O God, because of your unfailing love. Because of your great compassion, blot out the stain of my sins. Wash me clean from my guilt. Purify me from my sin. For I recognize my rebellion; it haunts me day and night. Against you, and you alone, have I sinned; I have done what is evil in your sight (Psalm 51:1–4).

*Forgiving God,
I am forgiven. I am forgiven. I am forgiven.
In hundreds of ways you tell me this.
Help me to know and to accept
that unqualified forgiveness. Amen.*

Chapter Thirty-Two
The Big-Time Operator

Yes, I know God's conception of time varies greatly from mine. Yes, I know the verse that says with the Lord a thousand years is as a day. Yes, I know God takes the long-term view of temporal events, and my view is necessarily limited.

Sure, I know all that; I just don't like it very much.

As I've looked over my prayers in recent days, time plays a big role. I ask God to do something for me or for someone else. Once in a while I receive a wonderful sense of assurance that it's going to happen. Then what?

Right. The waiting starts. The waiting goes on ... and on.

When I pause to think about it, I'm right in line with the saints of old. Here are four examples.

First, when Abraham is seventy-five, God promises him a son. The man waits *twenty-five years*.

Second, Joseph receives dreams from God that assure him he's going to be the head man and his family will bow to him. From the time his big brothers throw him into a pit until the promise unfolds, something like twenty years transpires.

Third, Samuel secretly anoints David as the new king of Israel. The secrecy—or so it seems to me—implies haste. About forty years later, David finally receives his crown over Jerusalem. Then he waits another seven years until he becomes king of the entire nation.

Fourth, God tells Paul at his conversion that he will speak to kings. Nice wait for Paul. For three years he goes into the desert to get himself theologically straight. Then he waits another dozen years before he speaks to his first king.

Even knowing those examples, I've still begged, pleaded, and sometimes all but demanded that God do something *now*. However, it doesn't seem to have speeded up the divine time frame.

Over the years, I've learned a little about waiting, but not much. I still want God to answer my prayers, if not instantly, at least quickly.

Occasionally I've asked God to do things and said, "And please, do it by January 28." A few times God honored that request; most of the time, the Maker of Time has ignored my deadlines.

I've tried to connect with the Big-Time Operator on this issue. But we can't seem to find a point of agreement. I've tried every form of persuasion and manipulation I'm capable of. None of my methods work.

I'm finally learning—still in the beginning stage—to accept temporal things under the direction of the Big-Time Operator.

Here's one incident. One day I felt overwhelmed with more things to do than I could possibly get done within the next twenty-four hours. "Help me, God," I asked. "I have to figure out some way to juggle all these time demands."

Then, just as clear as if an audible voice had spoken, the Big-Time Operator whispered, "You have time to do everything you *need* to do."

How could I argue with that voice? The emphasis was on the word *need*. And that's where I focused.

I hear people who complain about "the tyranny of the urgent." That's how I had felt. Urgent things crowded all around me. Many of them weren't important; some I could choose to put off a day or two. I made a few decisions about how to respond to the screaming demands, and I actually did have enough time to do what I really had to accomplish that day. I felt better at the end of the day.

The urgent cries often creep up on me. The louder they get, the more I'm convinced I need to obey the frenzied cries and obey *now*. From time to time I still need to remind myself of that statement: "You have time to do everything you *need* to do."

Another area the Big-Time Operator and I wrestle with is God's slow counting, or so it seems to me. A preacher once told me, "God is never in a hurry, but he's always on time." Great answer, but not very comforting when I'm praying, "Hurry up, God, hurry up." I struggle to accept God's concept of "on time."

Whenever I approach the Big-Time Operator, I have my watch and calendar firmly in mind. I want dates and times, but God refuses to be pinned down.

So what do I do?

I know what Abraham did. He waited twelve years, didn't see God's fulfillment take place, so he took Hagar as a concubine, a kind of second-class wife, impregnated her and got his son that way. But God said, "Sorry, Abe, that's not the son I meant. You have to wait a little longer." Another twelve years passed before the birth of Isaac.

So I know I don't want to take things into my own hands—at least not anymore. My mistake has been rushing ahead of God, and it has caused me a lot of problems. I'm a little more cautious than I used to be. I'm willing to wait, but it's a matter of ongoing prayer for me.

The other day I got really anxious about a personal matter for which I had been praying since 1985. I remembered a friend once said, "You know, in ten thousand years, you won't even remember this." The principle she wanted me to get, I think, was that the things I sweat today are soon forgotten.

I got a glimpse of this by reading through my old journals. I've been keeping yearly journals since 1972. It's painful to read pages of overwrought anxiety and concern. I agonized over one item in particular in my journal for over two weeks, every day. I had to laugh as I read it.

First, I had long forgotten the situation. Second, in 1978, it had seemed to be a life-or-death decision.

Now it seems rather trivial. I felt embarrassed that I had allowed myself to get so worked up about a situation that I couldn't remember twenty years later.

As I review my past, I see how the Big-Time Operator worked in me, trying to teach me patience. When I was sixteen and wanted to date Lois, who turned me down, I had no way of knowing that I'd find the perfect wife years later after I had turned to Jesus Christ. When I felt God speak to me about going to Africa, I couldn't know that I would wait four years. My list is virtually endless. Unfortunately, I catch on slowly.

For me, the time factor comes down to two things. First, it's all right to ask. In many ways, I'm still the little kid who talks to Big Daddy, the Abba Father. I have no way of knowing how granting my request will affect anything else. How would I know that Abba Father has too much wisdom to give me what I want, or to give it to me then? But I still ask.

Second, it really is a matter of trust. A few times when I've asked and not received, especially when I had a calendar deadline, my spirits have plummeted. Many times I never did see a reason for something turning out the way it did, especially when I ended up getting a big *no* from God.

But my faith says, "God loves me; God loves the whole world; God does what is right and at the right time." I may not always like the way the Big-Time Operator functions in my world, but I love God enough that I'm learning to accept it with gratitude.

But I am trusting you, O LORD, saying, "You are my God!" My future is in your hands (Psalm 31:14–15).

Big-Time Operator,
when I try to think of all the timing you're involved in
every hour of every day around the universe,
it goes beyond my comprehension.
When it comes to temporal matters,
I don't understand your timetable.
I do understand, though,
that you love me, and you don't withhold what I need.
That's enough for me to understand. Amen.

Chapter Thirty-Three
The Comforter

Life hurts. In hundreds of ways—through disappointments, sicknesses, losses, betrayals, or financial reverses—all of us feel the hurts of life.

Remember when your best friend turned on you and said something such as, "Just stay out of my life"? Or how about the time you studied hard and still didn't pass the exam? She would have been your first child, but you miscarried? You liked your job, worked faithfully, expected a promotion, but lost out to a coworker?

The pain seeps deep down inside. Some of us can let the tears flow and find relief. Others long ago learned, "Only sissies cry. Real men don't feel those things."

One spring day, I was reading in the tiny book of Lamentations. With image after image, the writer describes his suffering. But more than that. He insists that God is responsible for it. The Old Testament writers weren't afraid to call God the author of tragedy. It wasn't a wail of blame, but an acknowledgment of God as the ultimate cause of everything that goes on in the world.

They didn't say, "God allowed it to happen" or "God permitted it." They stated, "God did it." For example in chapter three:

1. "He has led me into darkness, shutting out all light" (v. 2).
2. "He has turned his hand against me again and again, all day long" (v. 3).
3. "He has made my skin and flesh grow old. He has broken my bones" (v. 4).
4. "He has besieged me and surrounded me with anguish and distress" (v. 5).
5. "He has buried me in a dark place, like those long dead" (v. 6).

I read those verses at a time when I felt some of the pangs of the writer. Frankly, my problems didn't compare with his. He lived in the final days of Jerusalem before the Babylonians carried his people into exile. Throughout the five chapters, he groans about his own suffering and that of his people.

As I read, I felt the depression of his words. It was as if the writer had allowed me to overhear his deepest, inmost thoughts. He pointed to God as the cause of all his difficulties. That day I too felt as if God had afflicted me, sent me into darkness and filled me with bitterness.

I read most of chapter three again, this time aloud. I resonated with the writer's pain and anguish. I felt as if I too were living in the darkness, or as 3:7 puts it, "He has walled me in, and I cannot escape."

As I continued to read chapter three, the tone began to change: "The thought of my suffering ... Yet I still dare to hope when I remember this: The faithful love of the LORD never ends! His mercies never cease" (19, 21–22). Finally comes the big leap of faith—he goes for comfort to the very God who had afflicted him. "The LORD is good to those who depend on him, to those who search for him. So it is good to wait quietly for salvation from the LORD" (3:25–26).

What a picture to contemplate. Assuming that it begins with our failure, we encounter the heavy hand of God. We cry out, "Help me. Don't turn your back." And then we go on to say that the God who brought the pain is the one who brings comfort.

Then we grasp the loving, comforting God, who is there all along. The Lamenter saw God as pushing him to despair before revealing joy and goodness.

God loves us enough to push us into a corner, to make us face our utter misery. Only after we've confronted our misery can we appreciate the comfort. Only after we've experienced the deepest darkness can we value the light.

> Though he [the LORD] brings grief, he also shows compassion because of the greatness of his unfailing love. For he does not enjoy hurting people or causing them sorrow (Lamentations 3:32–33).

Then why should we, mere humans, complain when we are punished for our sins? Instead, let us test and examine our ways. Let us turn back to the LORD (Lamentations 3:39–40).

God who brings comfort,
help me in my affliction,
make me aware of your goodness and love,
so that I can turn from the wrong paths,
and know your comfort once again. Amen.

Chapter Thirty-Four
The Purifier

Malachi, the last of the writing prophets in the Old Testament, painted a double image of God in his third chapter. The "messenger of the covenant" in verse one refers to Jesus Christ and sets the context for his coming: "... For he will be like a blazing fire that refines metal, or like a strong soap that bleaches clothes" (Malachi 3:2).

First, Jesus is revealed as a refiner of precious metals. The hot fire removes all impurities from silver and gold. The second picture is of Jesus as a fuller. That's a launderer whose soap makes garments white.

The two metaphors illustrate the double thrust of the purpose of the coming of Jesus. Malachi stresses that it's time to get cleaned up. And we need to heed the message today as much as the people of Malachi's time did.

He comes to purify the faithful and to eliminate the unfaithful. After the purification, the worship of the chosen people will once again be acceptable to God.

As I think of those two images, my perception is that purification would be a painful ordeal, something I would rather avoid.

What would it take, I wonder, for God to make me "white like snow"? I'm not talking about the usual meaning we attach, giving us salvation and cleansing our hearts. This passage refers to what we experience *after* coming to Christ. It's what we theologically call sanctification, or setting apart.

The refining image sounds terrible to me. It's a picture Peter uses in his first letter. Although he writes out of his experiences of being persecuted, he doesn't lay the blame on outside forces. This is God at work in us, he says, and if we follow Jesus Christ, we're going to be refined. That's part of the preparation for eternity.

It reminds me of a devotional message I read many years ago by long-ago missionary to India, Amy Carmichael. She wrote about Nazirites, men in the Old Testament who vowed to live ascetic lives. One of their restrictions was that they could not eat grapes or drink wine. Carmichael asked, "What, no raisins?" They were denied even the simple pleasures of life. As Nazirites they were in a special relationship of total commitment to God and lived by strict laws.

I wonder if God has called us to be spiritual Nazirites. By that, I mean it becomes a matter of "others may, you may not." It's not that we set legalistic demands for others or ourselves. But it does mean that we *voluntarily* allow God to treat us more strictly than people around us. If we're truly spiritual Nazirites, we are living in the ongoing refining fire.

It's such a strange paradox. God gradually restricts our lives and shuts out what others might accept as ordinary pleasures. Yet the restrictive life is richer, fuller, and more enjoyable.

Most of the refining happens in silence and out of the public view. The people I consider the most spiritual—that is, the most purified—don't speak of their trials or their purifying. They submit to God's cleansing, but it happens in such a private way that only two people know about it: God and the person involved.

Something about that appeals to me, that is, until I'm the person involved. Then I hear myself ask, "Why can't I have a handful of raisins?"

The God who wants to sanctify or set us apart for specific divine purposes doesn't demand or lay heavy laws on us. We voluntarily assume the load.

As we listen for the divine whisper of guidance, our lives change. It comes as a challenge, maybe as a suggestion, but always to purify us. I think of it as a whisper, and when we respond, we change.

As we ask God for the purifying fire in our lives, we acknowledge that it's a highly individual matter. If God takes away our raisins, it doesn't mean that no one else can eat them. It's simply a choice made by us in obedience to the Spirit of Purification.

I've read about people who've welcomed purification, persecution, and hardships because they believe that they are living the way the Lord lived. I'm not quite there, and I don't know if I'll ever have that kind of therapeutic outlook on suffering. But still—with trepidation—I ask God to continue to purify my life.

Many of us have no sense of nearing the station of Full Spirituality. In fact, when we look back at our progress, it's as if we've scarcely moved forward. "All these years, Lord, and this is all the progress I've made?"

Maybe it's because we can't see ourselves objectively. But we can see the refining fire. Even if we could see our progress, the Messenger of the Covenant is cleansing us in dozens of little ways. Maybe we're more sensitive about the words we speak and the tone of voice we use. Or maybe Jesus is softening the anger that lurks within us.

Because our needs are so different, and our impurities so diverse, who can set up a formula for anyone else? The secret—if there is one—is in listening to that soft whisper and saying, "Lord Jesus, it hurts when you scrub away at me, but thank you for caring enough to do it."

On one of my long prayer walks, after I had complained about the purifying process going on in my life, I realized that I was blessed by God. Right! *Blessed!* It means God cares enough to keep working with me. It reminds me that God still isn't through with me.

As I meditated along that line, a quiet joy filled my soul. "Yes, it's all right," I said to God. "Do it."

Dear friends, don't be surprised at the fiery trials you are going through, as if something strange were happening to you. Instead, be very glad—for these trials make you partners with Christ in his suffering, so that you will have the wonderful joy of seeing his glory when it is revealed to all the world (1 Peter 4:12–13).

Divine Purifier,
forgive me for pulling back,
for resisting the refining process.
Give me the grace to surge forward joyfully,
knowing that you are purifying me. Amen.

Chapter Thirty-Five
The Prayer Expert

I've read dozens of books on prayer, and I've learned a few things. But most of what I know about prayer, I've learned from the Prayer Expert. Since Jesus invented it and taught it, who would know more about prayer?

Twenty-three times the Gospels refer to Jesus praying, which means he prayed frequently, often silently and sometimes secretly. He prayed for himself and his mission, and he also prayed for his followers, for the sick, for Jerusalem, for the world, and for those in need. In short, he faithfully practiced the very thing he invented.

Luke's Gospel relates how he taught his followers to pray. It reads: Once Jesus was in a certain place praying. As he finished, one of his disciples came to him and said, "Lord, teach us to pray, just as John taught his disciples." Jesus said, "This is how you should pray: 'Father, may your name be kept holy. May your Kingdom come soon'" (Luke 11:1–2).

The model that follows is what we call the Lord's Prayer. The disciples may have meant they wanted Jesus to teach them a formulaic prayer. John the Baptist apparently gave his followers a model, and so did other religious leaders. In modern denominations, some congregations pray the Lord's Prayer at virtually every service. Others don't feel the need to repeat it literally, but take it as an example of the kind of praying we're to do.

What's noteworthy is that the disciples went to the Prayer Expert. After all, they had followed him, observed him in action, and decided they liked what they saw.

It's often helpful to consult the expert. When I first realized I needed a computer in 1983, I didn't know anything about them. So Paul Price, an early geek-expert, helped me get started. Within a few days, he taught me everything I needed to know. Since then, whenever I've decided to upgrade, I've gone to an expert for advice and instruction.

When it comes to prayer, there is really only one Expert, and whatever we know about prayer (if it's accurate information) comes from him.

After all the years of praying seriously, I still don't think of myself as an expert. I'm still learning. I'm not trying to devise the perfect seven words that unlock the whole universe. I'm trying to learn more about God, about me, and about how to open myself in prayer.

My attitude toward prayer has changed drastically over the years. Back in the early days after my conversion, if anyone had asked, I would have told them that prayer was simply talking with God. In fact, I think I said that a few times. Yet as I look back, I realize those early attempts were mostly begging sessions. I worked hard at convincing God to hear me and give me what I asked for. Without realizing it, I was trying to sell God on responding to me.

That's not where I am now. Asking is still a big part of prayer, but I've also learned other aspects, such as fellowship and praise.

I still wonder about how to pray specifically for particular needs. For instance, I have two good friends that I'll call Mike and John. I don't know how to pray for Mike. At age thirty-five, he's still trying to resolve identity issues that he talked about seven years ago. I don't like the catchall, "God, bless Mike," and I don't want to recite a list of ten things I think Mike needs right now. So how do I pray?

John, an ordained minister and former pastor, is one of the neediest people I know. If anyone yearns to be loved and valued for himself, that's John. How do I pray for him? Should I enumerate his needs one by one? Do I pick out one and stay with it until God answers before I move on to the second? How do I know which is most important?

I've committed myself to pray for both of these men daily. Mike knows that; I'm not sure John does. I'm not praying so they'll know. I'm praying because I genuinely care about both of them. Even so, I don't know how to pray effectively for them.

It's also frustrating that, after years of holding them up to God, I can't see any change. I wonder how many times I've paused in praying for those two men and said, "God, I just don't know how to pray." I'm not aware of their real needs—I see only outward behavior and character flaws.

How, Lord? How do I pray?

A few mornings ago, I walked through the woods with Mike on my mind. I had spoken to him on the phone the night before for nearly twenty minutes. I tried to focus my prayers for him but felt confused. I paused to lean against a black oak. "God, I don't have the slightest idea how to pray for Mike. Show me."

For several seconds, silence surrounded me. Then I heard myself saying, "Lord, won't you wrap your arms around Mike so that he'll know he's loved? Today, make him aware that you're with him and that you care deeply."

Simple stuff. Nothing profound or brilliant. But it came from my heart—something the Prayer Expert has taught me.

I could cite a variety of examples of what I've learned from the Prayer Expert. I'm still not sure I get it right, and I have a lot more to learn. It's like the lessons Paul Price gave me when I operated my first computer. I made mistakes even after he explained what I was supposed to do. But I kept at it. Now I can handle increasingly sophisticated computers. Even so, I know very little.

The best lesson I learned was to go to the expert when I have a problem.

The expert knows.

And the Prayer Expert not only knows how, but patiently works with me and teaches me. The Prayer Expert loves me and cares about my growth.

> Once Jesus was in a certain place praying. As he finished, one of his disciples came to him and said, "Lord, teach us to pray, just as John taught his disciples." Jesus said, "This is how you should pray: ..." (Luke 11:1–2).

Prayer Expert,
it sounds so simple to ask you to teach me to pray.
It gets complicated when I put it into practice.
Help me to keep praying,
to keep asking you for help,
and most of all,
to love you and those for whom I pray. Amen.

Chapter Thirty-Six
The Intercessor

Jesus prays for *me.*
That concept troubles me.
I can envision Jesus as my Friend, my Owner, my Savior, and dozens of other pictures. But when I try to think of Jesus *praying for me,* the information doesn't quite compute.

Yet the seventh chapter of Hebrews makes the image quite plain. In that section of the letter, the writer compares Jesus with the high priests of the Old Testament. Once a year, on the Day of Atonement, the high priest offered an animal sacrifice, confessed the sins of the people, and prayed for Israel. Those priests had to do it every year. Jesus, however, did his work once and it lasts through eternity.

There's more: "But because Jesus lives forever, his priesthood lasts forever. Therefore he is able, once and forever, to save those who come to God through him. He lives forever to intercede with God on their behalf" (Hebrews 7:24–25). I have read those verses in Greek as well as in various English translations, but the words hit me only recently. Jesus "lives forever to intercede" for us. It's not a once-for-all event like his death on the cross. I understand the Innocent One giving his life for us, the guilty, at the cross—a one-time act. But how do I grasp the concept of the ongoing intercession of Jesus for me? For us?

In his *function* as high priest, Jesus, the sinless one, continues to pray to the Eternal Father for us. Somehow in a way that's beyond my intellectual comprehension (although I accept it by faith), Jesus, who is also God, is interceding with another part of himself for us. The only way my limited mind can make sense of this is simply to think of Jesus, who is now in the presence of God, functioning in his role as high priest. He's still praying on our behalf, *even this minute.*

The closest I can get to understanding the constant intercession of Jesus is to reflect on my old Sunday school teacher, Marie Garbie, whom I've mentioned elsewhere. For at least ten years, from the day I quit Sunday school as a child until I visited her after my conversion, she prayed for me every day.

It amazes me that during all my years of living away from God, one woman talked to God about me every day. Even though I had no awareness of her prayers (nor did I care), she didn't stop. She was a priest for me. She told me that she didn't just mention my name, but "I wrestled with the devil for your soul," she said.

So I understand the matter of true and deep intercession. But Jesus praying for me? Praying for me and for all the other individuals through the centuries? It's beyond my capacity to grasp.

At the same time, it touches me to realize that Jesus didn't merely give himself as an eternal offering and then the work was done. He's still at it, still doing his priestly duty.

The apostle Paul writes of the goodness and the severity of God in the King James Version of Romans 11:22. The New International Version translates it as the "kindness and sternness of God." The New Living Translation says, "... He is severe toward those who disobeyed, but kind to you if you continue to trust in his kindness ..." That's where Jesus stands—between those two extremes. He wants the kindness of God for all, and prays for us so that we won't have to feel God's severity.

What a thought!

Jesus prays for me. Always.

Today when I went for my six-miles run, I kept thinking, Lord Jesus, you're praying for me right now. You're praying *right now*. It gave me a sense of deep comfort to think that at all times, at every moment in time, Jesus is talking to God on my behalf. I don't know how Jesus does it or what he says, but I know he prays that Cec will do the correct thing or make the righteous choice.

He prays *for me*.

He also prays for you.

⚜ ⚜ ⚜

[Jesus prayed in the garden of Gethsemane,] "I have revealed you to the ones you gave me from this world. They were always yours. You gave them to me, and they have kept your word. Now they know that everything I have is a gift from you, for I have passed on to them the message you gave me. They accepted it and know that I came from you, and they believe you sent me. My prayer is not for the world, but for those you have given me, because they belong to you" (John 17:6–9).

Jesus Christ, my Intercessor,
you are praying for me,
your love is showing itself—
your protective hand,
your loving guidance.
Thank you. Amen.

Chapter Thirty-Seven
The Compassionate One

It's not strange to think about Jesus as the Compassionate One. Look at all the healings he performed. Even four-year-old kids can sing "Jesus Loves Me."

As strange as it may sound, though, I didn't consciously connect Jesus' love with compassion until recently. In the New Testament the Greek word for God's love is *agape* and the word has nothing to do with emotions. It's an attitude, a commitment, a form of behavior.

It took me a long time to understand Christians who said, "I love you, but I don't like you." For me, one encompassed the other. Gradually a marvelous reality dawned on me: godly love—love in its purest form—doesn't involve feelings. Love is a commitment.

I learned this a few years ago when I had a few hassles with a member of our church, whom I'll call Pete. In business meetings, I could count on Pete's taking an opposing stand on anything I said. We simply had different value systems and we viewed life differently.

One day I was in a low spot after a run-in with Pete. Then Betty, one of the sweetest women in the congregation, called me. She had been trying to deal with a man named Bob who wasn't easy to like, hadn't had much of a happy life, felt rejected by most people, and worst of all, just didn't seem to have much common sense.

I quoted the words from a sign I had (and still have) on my office wall: "People need love the most when they deserve it the least." I threw in the biblical reference about Jesus rebuking those who behave kindly only to those who respond to them. Same message. Then I had the good sense to shut up.

After a long pause, Betty thanked me. "I don't love him like a brother in the Lord," she said. "You know, I've never opened my heart to him. That's what I need to do."

After that conversation, I sat at my desk and I heard an inner question, *Did you hear what you said to Betty?*

Was that God speaking through my mind? Probably, and I wasn't going to ignore it. Mentally, I replayed what I had just said. Then I got the message. Pete didn't deserve my love—or so it seemed to me—but he sure needed it.

I repented. I prayed for Pete regularly for a long time. We never got to be friends, but I no longer bristled around him. (Of course, actually, I think he softened.)

That's how I began to think of love—objectively doing the right thing for others, reaching out to people regardless of feelings. Love means caring for their welfare.

Consequently, that's how I perceived God—magnanimously enduring us, but not necessarily liking it. Lately, I've begun to catch a broader view of the divine personality, to see that Jesus Christ is compassionate. That is, Jesus *feels* loving. He cares.

Yeah, simple, I know, as most things about the divine nature are when we get them figured out. In times before, I had explained John 11:35 ("Then Jesus wept") by saying: "Hey, he wept for Lazarus because he was a friend." That didn't necessarily mean Jesus would *feel* sadness for me or anyone else. I also knew that the Gospel writer says, "Looking at the man, [the rich young ruler], Jesus felt genuine love for him" (Mark 10:21). But he used the Greek verbal form of *agape,* so it didn't have to refer to emotion, but commitment to the young man's good.

Then just today I read this verse: "And when Jesus went out He saw a great multitude; and He was moved with compassion for them, and healed their sick" (Matthew 14:14, NKJV).

Here's another statement: "And Jesus went about all the cities and villages, teaching in their synagogues, preaching the gospel of the kingdom, and healing every sickness and every disease among the people. But when He saw the multitudes, He was moved with compassion for them, because they were weary and scattered, like sheep having no shepherd"

(Matthew 9:35–36, NKJV). Jesus cared *emotionally*; his actions involved his feelings. The plight of the crowd touched some powerful emotional chord in him. Then I saw Jesus the Compassionate One. He cared for the multitude. Does that mean he cares for me?

As I prayed today, I tried to think of myself as the object of God's compassion. What would it be like to be the object of the caring emotions of my Savior?

Tears came to my eyes as I realized this was more than what we call disinterested love. This was a love that embodies concern, feelings, and understanding.

"Do you really have those warm, caring feelings for me?" I asked.

I remained silent, and slowly, like a warmth that spread through me, I *felt* loved. God's compassion engulfed me. I felt like a small child again, being held tightly in my mothers' arms.

Then another idea crept into my consciousness: *If God is that compassionate toward you, shouldn't you be as tender and compassionate toward yourself?*

I couldn't believe my own thought. Compassionate toward *myself*? What did that mean?

As I allowed the silence to remain, I did one of those quick life inventories. Yes, I had been a bit hard on myself. Yes, I had demanded much and, no, I hadn't been particularly understanding when I failed.

I continued to resist those thoughts, and the moments ticked by. Finally, a memory came to me. In the late 1980s, I had a prayer partner named Bob

Ramey. One day he told me, "You're understanding and compassionate with others. Why don't you turn a little of it on yourself?"

I stared at him in shock.

"Think of yourself objectively. If Cec were another person, someone who came to you for help, how would you feel toward him?"

"I get it now," I said. Unfortunately, I soon forgot the lesson. A full decade later, the memory crashed inside my head. I started accepting and applying truths I had perceived all along on an intellectual plane, but had never allowed to creep into my heart.

Now I know that I can be understanding, accepting, and compassionate toward even Cec because of Jesus Christ. To follow him means to be like him, to love and care about what he cares about. And Cec is a person he cares about.

This must sound like one of the simplest things I've ever written. And it is. But it's a lesson that was a long time getting through to me. I've finally accepted the *personal* compassion of a compassionate God.

Today, I've meditated on the Compassionate One—the one who understands. It's as if Jesus' arm is around my shoulder and he whispers, "It's okay to be less than perfect. I care deeply about you."

Then I know I'm in the presence of the Compassionate One.

⚜ ⚜ ⚜

Give all your worries and cares to God,
for he cares about you (1 Peter 5:7).

*Compassionate One,
thank you for loving me with an emotional love;
thank you that your heart is touched with my pain,
my heartaches,
my disappointments.
You care. You really care. Thanks. Amen.*

Chapter Thirty-Eight
My Helper

"I'm a carpenter's helper," he said. He had finished high school three months earlier, and it was his first full-time job.

As we talked, I thought about his using the term *helper*. In recent years, various occupations have added that particular word as a job designation, such as a teacher's aide. It usually means they do the grunt work, the kind of leftover or unpleasant tasks those higher up the success ladder don't want to do. They're the "gofers" in the world.

This morning, by contrast, I read John 14:26 in the New King James Version, translated in 1979. As I read, it made me realize how much language has changed in the past twenty years. Take the first part of that verse. Jesus said to his disciples, "But the Helper, the Holy Spirit, whom the Father will send in My name ..." As the rest of the verse and the context show, the Helper here has quite a different task than being some kind of Divine Gofer.

Maybe, I thought, that's part of the problem. We have put a modern meaning to a word and applied it here in a way that God never intended. We have tried—innocently or foolishly—to make the Holy Spirit become our private gofer. It's as if we see that the Spirit's purpose is to further *our* plans, and do the cleanup work for us. Or to put it in the practical way in which many of us operate, we pray, get no instant response. So we decide what we want to do, we pray for the Spirit *to help us*, and we boldly go forward to do the task.

That procedure makes us forget who's in charge. It's much too easy for us to decide we know the right things to do at the proper time, or to delude ourselves into believing our task is to control our lives. Then, when we get into trouble, we know who's in charge because we cry out to God to come to our rescue. (This is the voice of experience speaking.)

If we read all of John 14:26, of course, we learn the purpose of the Helper: "He will teach you all things, and bring to your remembrance all things that I said to you."

There we have it. First, Jesus said the Holy Spirit becomes our Ally, our Friend, and our Helper, who will teach us all things. Obviously, Jesus wanted those disciples then, and us today, to know that we are always the learners and are always taking in understanding. It implies that none of us ever reaches the place where we have grasped and lived the whole truth.

Jesus' words, "Bring to your remembrance," say to me that once we know the words and pray for guidance, the Helper speaks. (We may have to wait, but the Helper does speak.) If we wait long enough, we may suddenly "remember" Jesus' words. A verse rings through our heads, and it's God dialing our number. If we're open, the Helper constantly reminds us of what Jesus said.

The first time I had such an experience, I was still fairly new in the faith, and I had an opportunity to speak to a secular group about career directions. I could think of a number of things I wanted to say about God and the Bible, but I thought, I can't talk that way in front of such an audience. I decided to make it a purely secular talk. Then I prayed and asked for God's guidance.

A partial verse came to me: "Not as though the Word of God hath taken no effect ..." (Romans 9:6 KJV). I heard, and I got the divine message. God was helping me. I had decided God's Word wouldn't be effective or helpful among nonbelievers. Now with new boldness and a reliance on the Divine Helper, I spoke easily about my conversion and how I felt God was directing my life.

I couldn't believe the response afterward. Almost everyone thanked me for telling them my story. None of them said, "Yeah, that's what I want," but no one seemed offended. I realized then that I had told them about me and hadn't told them they had to follow me or my path.

The Helper also interprets the words brought back to our minds. If we read some of Jesus' sayings as they appear on the page, they can leave us in confusion. For example, are we to take literally that *anything* we ask in his name we'll get? How many people literally cut off their hands? How many sell everything and give it to the poor?

The Divine Interpreter, the Holy Spirit, helps us understand what Jesus intended at the time he spoke and what he intends for the words to mean to us today.

In John chapter fifteen, we have some of the same language about the Spirit as Helper: "But when the Helper comes, whom I shall send to you from the Father, the Spirit of truth who proceeds from the Father, he will testify of me" (15:26, NIV).

The Spirit will testify or bear witness of Jesus. That's the purpose of the Helper in our lives—to make Jesus Christ more alive, more vital in our lives—but also to work in us as we daily live and work among others.

The Helper enables us to carry out God's will, instead of helping us to accomplish our goals.

Our role is to listen to the Helper.

> The Lord is my helper, so I will have no fear. What can mere people do to me? (Hebrews 13:6).

The Lord is for me, so I will have no fear. What can mere people do to me? (Psalm 118:6).

Divine Helper,
forgive me for trying to make you into someone
who helps me further my plans.
Teach me instead
to rely on you, the Helper,
so that I can further your plans. Amen.

Chapter Thirty-Nine
The One Who Holds Me Accountable

"I need someone to make me accountable," Jim Martin said.

He and I had known each other for a few months, but we had never talked seriously before. Then one day in 1976, we sat together at a luncheon meeting of local pastors. I was a Presbyterian and Jim was a Lutheran. Our churches were located a ten-minute drive from each other.

"I know I need someone who'll make me face myself and give account of my faithfulness to God." Jim then asked me to enter into a covenant with him.

I felt honored.

Jim struggled with reading his Bible every day and with not allowing "preacher things" to crowd out his devotional time. "I know that if I try to set aside time seven days a week, I'll fail," he said, "but for a start, I want to be able to commit myself to reading my Bible and having personal prayer time four days a week. When we meet, I want you to ask me if I did."

As much as possible for the next nine years, until Jim accepted a pastorate in Michigan, we met weekly. Both of us made our accountability session a top priority in our lives. Sometimes our meetings took place over lunch; many times we ran six miles together at noon instead of eating. Occasionally, we met at the end of a busy day. But we met faithfully. And we talked.

Jim and I learned a lot about each other over those nine years. Jim is about six feet, three inches tall; dark; blue-eyed; handsome, with one of those magic smiles; and quite articulate. When Jim hadn't been faithful, he didn't have to tell me. I could tell by his evasive tactics. After I caught on, however, I was able to cut through his defenses. Once I asked, "Jim, do you want to tell me or should I tell you?"

We laughed. Jim wanted me to be there for him, but it embarrassed him to say, "I didn't make it this week." More than once, he admitted, "Even though I know you understand and you're my friend, I feel as if I fail God and you when I don't live up to my commitment."

I had my share of spiritual failures as well. It wasn't any easier for me to confess to Jim than for him to open up to me. But we did it.

A few days ago while thinking about those days, I read the words of the apostle Paul about the concept of accountability. He wrote that he had visited the church leaders in Jerusalem to talk to them about his ministry. Apparently, they had limited their preaching to Jews, and Paul had reached out to non-Jews (Gentiles). He writes, "Then fourteen years later I went back to Jerusalem again, this time with Barnabas; and Titus came along, too. I went there because God revealed to me that I should go. While I was there I met privately with those considered to be leaders of the church and shared with them the message I had been preaching to the Gentiles. I wanted to make sure that we were in agreement, for fear that all my efforts had been wasted and I was running the race for nothing" (Galatians 2:1–2).

His words tell us that Paul went to the top men of the Church to make himself accountable. Or as one of my friends said, "It was Paul's reality check."

Even Jesus was concerned about the accountability. In defense of his ministry he said, "John [the Baptist] was like a burning and shining lamp, and you were excited for a while about his message. But I have a greater witness than John—my teachings and my miracles. The Father gave me these works to accomplish, and they prove that he sent me" (John 5:35–36).

Jesus tried to make them see that he had been accountable to God and had been found faithful. He didn't simply preach or do miracles, but he did only as his heavenly Father directed him. He was saying, "I've been accountable, and John is my witness."

I've also learned something myself about this matter of accountability. In the past, no matter how high I scored on my spiritual accomplishment report card, I had the sense that I should have done more. I should have tried harder.

I wonder if some of that is a result of our modern culture. I heard on the radio that a man had received a card from a business associate in Thailand. The card ended with the words, "And I wish you a busy life." The words perplexed the recipient until he realized that the third-world citizen had picked up something about Americans. We constantly grumble about how busy and harassed we are, and we say we have no idea how to cut down on our load. But that's not really true. Keeping busy makes us feel important. The busier we are, the more significant we feel.

I understand that card's message. For years having too many things going has been part of my problem with accountability. I've made myself busier than God intended me to be. Sometimes I've even decided to get "more spiritual" by increased reading and longer praying.

If those desires come out of genuine hunger or need, that's wonderful. But sometimes we decide it will make us more spiritual or more important or more rewarded in heaven. Maybe we even believe that God will love us a little more if we do more.

I wish I could say sincerely, "Well, Lord, I have been faithful in everything." Aside from the fact that such a statement smacks of pride, those are difficult words for me to speak. I'm constantly conscious of not measuring up. The words from the *Book of Common Worship* state my case too well: "We have followed too much the devices and desires of our own hearts.... We have left undone those things which we ought to have done; and we have done those things which we ought not to have done...."

Even when I feel I've had a good day spiritually and really tracked with Jesus Christ, a nagging voice inside whispers, "Yeah, but you could have done better."

Strange. When I talked today to the One Who Holds Me Accountable, I didn't hear the Bible verse, "Well done, my good and faithful servant" whispered (see Matthew 25:23). Neither did I hear, "Oh, Cec, you failed again. I'm disappointed in you." But I sensed God's pleasure that I want to live a life of commitment and accountability.

I ask God to make me accountable for my actions and for the way I use the hours of my day. At one time I was much like Jim, who expected some kind of rebuke, or maybe a lecture on how to get his act together. Yet the more I walk with God, the more I understand divine ways. Instead of rebuke, I receive acceptance and affirmation. Sometimes, it's true that I need to stir myself a bit. It's easy to get complacent in life. But I often pray, "God, I stop all the unnecessary business and give myself to you."

On my best days, when my energy is still high and I'm ready to go out and do everything again, and also on those days when I'm exhausted, I feel his hand on me and an inner voice says, "Be at peace. Rest."

So whether you eat or drink, or whatever you do, do it all for the glory of God (1 Corinthians 10:31).

God,
make me accountable to you for everything I do;
in giving my mind and my body rest.
Thank you for being such a loving Master. Amen.

Chapter Forty
The Mysterious Stranger

The road to Emmaus story has always intrigued me. After Jesus' resurrection, two disciples walk toward a small town about seven miles from Jerusalem. Along the way, a stranger joins them. The newcomer, seemingly ignorant of the events of the day, listens as the two men tell him about the crucifixion of Jesus and the report of his resurrection.

As they walk, the stranger begins to teach them. At sunset, they stop for a meal. In the "breaking of the bread," they realize they have been talking to Jesus all along. Then Jesus disappears (see Luke 24:13–35).

The story intrigues me for a number of reasons. First, I've never figured out why they didn't recognize Jesus. Even if he had some kind of heavenly body, he must have been the same shape and size. If nothing else, wouldn't they have known from the sound of his voice, or the way he spoke, the depth of his teaching, or the intensity of his words?

I understand the story on an experiential level though. I have encountered those mysterious strangers in my life—people God sends just to answer my prayers. They're unexpected messengers of God. I've listened to their message. Then, being totally in tune with the Holy Spirit, I say, "Ah, yes, this is God." Right?

Well, uh, not quite. I'm a bit dull at hearing God speak to me through mysterious strangers. I read my Bible and ask God to "enliven the Word," as we used to say in one church. Or I pray with a specific request and expect God to speak to me through impressions, doors opening or closing, or something happening.

Like many others, I've been praying and just then—like the proverbial lightning bolt—comes a moment of insight. That's God answering my prayer.

But through strangers? How can that be?

In the Old Testament, it happened. For instance, God calls Gideon to deliver the nation from the Midianites. But he is an illegitimate son in an insignificant clan of the tribe of Manasseh, and calls himself the least in the family. Who is he to do such things? In his insecurity and uncertainty, Gideon seeks guidance.

Most people know the fleece story. Gideon prays for God to work through signs. The first night he puts down a wool fleece on the threshing floor. He says, "If the dew is on the fleece but the floor itself remains dry, I'll know God is speaking to me." God gives him the answer he asks for.

The next night, Gideon reverses his request and in the morning the wool is dry but the ground is wet (see Judges 6:36–40). In the next chapter, Gideon and his servant, Purah, go to the edge of the enemy camp. They hear soldiers on guard duty:

> Gideon crept up just as a man was telling his companion about a dream. The man said, 'I had this dream, and in my dream a loaf of barley bread came tumbling down into the Midianite camp. It hit a tent, turned it over, and knocked it flat!' His companion answered, 'Your dream can mean only one thing—God has given Gideon son of Joash, the Israelite, victory over Midian and all its allies!' When Gideon heard the dream and its interpretation, he bowed in worship before the LORD (Judges 7:13–15).

God spoke the truth—and gave guidance—through a heathen soldier. Wasn't that like a mysterious stranger? It was a voice of God that Gideon had never expected.

Those mysterious strangers have come my way more often than I may have realized. They are answered prayers and often I don't realize it. Or I figure it out much later.

Yet, increasingly, I hear the divine whisper (and it's usually a whisper instead of a shout) that comes to me from the most unlikely lips. One day, I was grumbling about all the projects I had going and the small amount of time in which to do them. After a couple of minutes listening to me, a man—a casual acquaintance—smiled and said quietly, "You know, you don't have to save the world today. The less important things will wait until tomorrow."

In my frenzied state, I almost didn't hear the mysterious stranger speaking. In fact, I had my rebuttal already half-formed in my head (we compulsive people do that expertly), and then I stopped. He was absolutely right!

I didn't accomplish everything I had planned that day. But when I went to bed that night, I knew I had finished the important things I needed to do.

Another time, we were visiting a church and I didn't feel particularly comfortable with the style of worship. Even more distracting for me was that I was focusing on something going on inside me rather than on the service. I was struggling with a problem that had happened several years ago, and I realized I'd never fully shoved it into the past.

Just then the minister quoted Philippians 3:13, "... but I focus on this one thing: forgetting the past and looking forward to what lies ahead." Then he added, "Looking back means going back."

I jerked to attention. I felt as if that man had read my mind. Later, as I reflected, I realized it was one of those visits from the Mysterious Stranger.

My wife, Shirley, isn't exactly a mysterious stranger, but once in a while she takes on that role.

In her quiet way, she'll make an offhand comment that strikes me almost as if I'm listening to the final crescendo of the Hallelujah Chorus.

One more example. I usher at the early service. One Sunday morning I went into a nervous frenzy. I couldn't find the bulletins, the flowers weren't on the altar, and my classroom had not been set up properly for me to teach immediately after the service. Just then, a woman came in early, looked at me and said, "Hmm, your god must have died last night."

"What?" I asked.

"Every time I've come here, you've been warm and smiling. Today, you're a picture of gloom. I thought maybe your god had died."

"Nope," I said, "I'm the one. Only I'm not dead, just marginally terminal." And I laughed, but just then I heard the voice of the Mysterious Stranger.

I don't know when the Mysterious Stranger is going to come. I hear voices around me all the time, especially those that want to direct my life or cure me of some kind of character flaw. Like yesterday morning I spoke with Mike on the phone about a situation I was dealing with.

"I know a first-class therapist," he said. "She sure has helped me." For several minutes he tried to sell me on her.

I thanked Mike, and I knew he meant well, but as I prayed, I knew it simply wasn't the voice of the Mysterious Stranger. I'm not opposed to therapists, but I'm a stubborn independent who works things out internally. I couldn't hear someone else's Mysterious Stranger. I have to hear my own.

So how do I recognize the Mysterious Stranger? I don't always. I suspect the Stranger has whispered 23,431 times in my life when I haven't gotten the message.

When I do hear, however, it's like a pager going off or the alarm pulling me out of deep sleep. It's like a voice that says, "Ah, ha" and I feel a jab in my stomach. The internal witness says, "This is an ordinary human being, but God has just used her to tell you what you need to hear right now."

As I pray, I ask God to keep me open to divine appearances in the form of the Mysterious Stranger. I want to hear God speak through a child's smile, a grandmother's embrace, the words of a hymn, or even someone who doesn't like me.

The Mysterious Stranger is around, and I've committed myself to develop a listening ear.

> [One of the men on the road to Emmaus said,] "Didn't our hearts burn within us as he talked with us on the road and explained the Scriptures to us?" (Luke 24:32).

Mysterious God,
speak to me through the Bible,
or with a word from friends or people I don't know.
Use your voice as the Mysterious Stranger,
but most of all,
speak to me,
and when I hear you,
enable me to whisper, "Ah, yes." Amen.

Chapter Forty-One
The God of Whispers

Visualize the concept of God working in human lives. What image do you come up with? Do you see Peter preaching to thousands on the day of Pentecost? Jesus teaching the multitudes? Moses at Mount Sinai?

Do you see Joshua leading the charge around Jericho? King David defeating the enemy armies? Or is it Jesus restoring a man's withered arm? Peter touching a dead woman named Tabitha and restoring her to life?

Those were all instances when God worked. Some are more impressive than others, of course, but who could say which is more important? In the events of ongoing life, we can say, "Oh, well, it would have happened anyway." Or we can discern God's activity and proclaim, "It was a miracle!"

As I continue my own adventures with prayer, I'm trying to discern the miraculous hand of God at work. Such divine interventions happen in many ways. It could be the timing of events. Or it could be that someone said or did the right thing when it was most needed. Maybe an elder prayed for a seriously ill church member who recovered.

There is one way God works that many of us tend to ignore. It's when God whispers. I noticed this in an odd story in 1 Kings chapter eighteen. A rugged prophet named Elijah confronts 450 prophets of the idol Baal on Mount Carmel. He challenges them to prepare a sacrifice and pray for Baal to appear from heaven and burn their sacrifice. They pray, scream, and cut themselves while Elijah taunts. No answer comes and they give up. Then it's Elijah's turn. He orders water thrown on the sacrifice before he prays. Immediately, fire comes from heaven and licks up the sacrifice.

Isn't that a great victory and triumph for God's people? But that's not the end of the story. The wicked queen threatens Elijah's life. Elijah is worn out, so he runs. Eventually, he hides in a cave. And that's where God's whisper comes in.

Here's the way the New Revised Standard Version (NRSV) translates the story:

> He [God] said, "Go out and stand on the mountain before the Lord, for the Lord is about to pass by." Now there was a great wind, so strong that it was splitting mountains and breaking rocks in pieces before the Lord, but the Lord was not in the wind; and after the wind an earthquake, but the Lord was not in the earthquake; and

> after the earthquake a fire, but the LORD was not in the fire; and after the fire a sound of sheer silence. When Elijah heard it, he wrapped his face in his mantle and went out and stood at the entrance of the cave. Then there came a voice to him that said, "What are you doing here, Elijah?" (1 Kings 19:11–13).

Elijah expects God to come with drama and noise. Instead God comes in what several translations call the "still small voice." The NRSV gets closest to the Hebrew, and it could be translated, "the sound of a gentle stillness."

The prophet feels the presence of God in the quietness. A sense of fear and wonder hangs over him and he covers his face in reverence. The earthquake has shaken the earth's foundations, the fire has fallen from heaven. And both of them must have been impressive and powerful. Although Elijah has witnessed God's activities, he isn't hearing God's voice.

Only in the awe of stillness does he feel overwhelmed and cover his face as if he were afraid to look on the glory of God.

Whatever God said in the cave, the writer found it impossible to put into words. It was obviously one of those times when the experience went beyond human expression. One scholar said, "The voice of silence spoke."

I understand that term, because I've experienced that voice of silence—except that it's not really silent. It communicates. It penetrates somewhere deep inside. That's why I call it the whisper of God. It comes in those moments as an "audible silence."

I prefer God to communicate through activity, through events, through visible evidence. I like being active, on the go, and always involved in something. I'm part of that personality type who gets things done, runs fast, and stays involved in a lot of activity.

I'm like many believers. We're prone to believe only in the whirlwind, the earthquake, and the fire. Sometimes we even try to help God make those things happen. We want to advance the kingdom of God. We tend to assume that God's not working unless life happens on a large scale.

If our church had only two new members last year, obviously we weren't as effective as the megachurch four miles away that took in over a thousand. If our personal giving doesn't measure up to the percentage of the top givers, we must be holding back on God. We look for the spectacular, conclusive signs of God's mighty revolutionary energy. God does work and paint on gigantic canvases—sometimes. But it's only one way.

Sometimes God forces us into caves as he did Elijah, so we can hear the quietness of God—the whisper.

In recent years, however, the whisper of God has nudged me to listen more, and to hold back and wait instead of jumping into activities, no matter how good they may appear.

I'm not contemplative by nature. I've tried to pray for a couple of hours at a time, and it just doesn't work with me. Try twenty minutes or a half hour. I'm not the kind who can kneel indefinitely in prayer without falling asleep. But it's disturbing to people like me when we realize that we're not getting enough bang for our bucks, or enough fireworks from our rockets.

"What's wrong, Lord?" we ask. "I thought I was doing your will."

When we get really frustrated, then we might listen—truly listen—and we might hear the whisper of God that comes in the silence.

Silence is important, but we need quiet spirits, quiet places, and quiet times. Even around noise and confusion we can find that quiet center.

I think I've figured out why the writer of 1 Kings had so much trouble expressing what happened in the cave. It was silent and it took place in utter solitude. My experience works this way. In utter quietness, away from the family, the TV, and the noise of the day, I can listen. For a short time, I can sit in contemplation. I try to clear my head of all the things I want to talk to God about or think about.

I take time to listen. Sometimes I do it by paying attention to my breathing. Other times I imagine my body as a big empty space and I wait for the Spirit of God to fill it.

Then—in those quiet moments—the silence of God comes to me. But silence needs expression. That silence, in ways I can't comprehend, translates into thoughts. I hear my own words, what I sometimes call my inner voice, but I prefer to call it God's whisper.

I have no formula to explain how and when God speaks in this way. I can't even be certain that it's God and not my own desires—I get them mixed up at times. But I can think of occasions when I heard the whisper so clearly that no one could have persuaded me it wasn't God.

One day I was walking in Chicago, in a reflective mood. Hardly aware of my surroundings, I was in the "waiting mode" and had been asking God for guidance. I looked up just then and saw a theater marquee with the film *Tanganyika* (now Tanzania), and that whisper said, "That's where you're going." I never doubted that I had heard God's whisper. Four years later, we went to Kenya, but we lived on the Tanganyika border and did much of our work in that country.

When it's the real whisper of God, we know on some deep level. "I know without knowing how I know," a friend once said of her experience. "But it's so certain, no one could talk me out of it."

That's the whisper I want to hear more regularly. As I pray and worship, I provide the Lord with an opportunity to whisper.

⚜ ⚜ ⚜

"Be still, and know that I am God!" (Psalm 46:10).

And after the fire there was the sound of a gentle whisper (1 Kings 19:12).

God,
whisper to me.
Teach me to listen in utter silence,
so that I may be ready,
alert,
and open to your silent whisper. Amen.

Chapter Forty-Two
The Weeping God

"God feels our pain with us," said dear old Mrs. Rodbro at the Wednesday evening prayer service. She had related an experience that took her through great agony, but she found peace because "God felt every heartache, every pain."

In my early twenties, I was a new convert and still learning the basics of the faith. That was the first time I heard anyone talking about God *feeling*. I could hardly grasp the significance of her testimony.

Old Testament writers refer to God's strong arm, eyes that see, ears that hear, the palm engraved with our names, as well as references to God's anger and displeasure. I learned that the Bible is filled with what we call *anthropomorphisms,* which literally means "human forms." The concept enabled the writers to explain the unexplainable.

Were Mrs. Rodbro's words, then, simply a metaphor to say that God condescends to us in our need? For me, it meant that God cared and acted on our behalf, but always from a distance. We benefit from the blessings of God, and because they affect us personally, we respond to them personally and emotionally. That sounded simple enough.

But that just didn't satisfy me. I remember thinking, Surely God doesn't have emotions. So if that's true, how can God "feel"?

Finally, I thought about Jesus, the human personification of God. He truly represents and models God for us, and he certainly had feelings.

Perhaps it sounds as if I'm making too much of the emotions of God. I'm writing about it because it troubled me for a long time. How could an all-powerful, all-knowing, sovereign God "feel" for humanity? I could grasp God acting benevolently as a rational decision, the way I might decide to donate money for victims of a flood or send underprivileged kids to camp.

But God feeling human emotions? God hurting emotionally?

I'm slightly embarrassed to write about this discovery—and it was a discovery to me. Long after I had intellectually grasped that God felt, it remained just that—an intellectual concept, a doctrine of the mind.

I know Jesus wept over Lazarus's death (see John 11:35). Even the witnesses commented on how much Jesus loved his friend. Another time, Jesus cried over Jerusalem (Luke 19:41) and its impending destruction. But I had read those passages many times before the fire struck and the heat inside said, "Ah, yes, I understand."

That's it. God weeps for us.

The experience that taught me about the Weeping God began when another Christian hurt me deeply. He spoke unkind words about me, privately to a few of my friends and then, later, publicly. I wasn't there to defend myself, and I heard about it only much later.

When I heard what he had said about me, I felt crushed. I went into the worst bout of depression I'd ever experienced. I cried, and I pleaded for God's help. Once I even prayed (scripturally, of course!) for God to "requite" him for his sins, a pious way of asking God to punish him for what he had done to me. Many times I asked God to forgive him and me.

I didn't get over the heartache. It stayed with me for weeks, often like a low-grade fever that surged with pain from time to time. At one point, I was sure I had gotten over it and forgiven him.

"I'm over it now," I said to my wife. "I've finally put it behind me."

But my wife, who knows me well, said, "If you've forgiven him, why do you keep bringing it up?"

She had me.

Back to prayer and more prayer. One rainy October night, Shirley was out of town, and I was home alone. I felt spiritually low. The man's name kept coming back to me, and I knew I had to break through my resistance and forgive him.

I prayed for several minutes and nothing happened. Then—and I have no explanation why it happened at that moment—I began to cry. It felt as if all the heartache and pain I had stored inside burst into the open. Resentment, anger, and jealousy filled my heart. I confessed and asked forgiveness, but the pain didn't go away.

"Don't you care?" I cried out to God at one point. "Can't you see how much I hurt?"

In one of those quiet, unexplainable moments, I knew God felt my pain. I knew, as I had never known experientially or emotionally before, that God felt what I was going through. It was no longer a distant caring or a commitment to give me peace, but a divine identification with a flawed human being.

The Weeping God, I thought. What a concept.

We talk of divine power, but how often do we talk about the Weeping God? The one who feels our infirmities with us? Immediately I thought of the book of Hebrews and its reference to Jesus as our high priest. "This High Priest of ours understands our weaknesses, for he faced all of the same testings we do, yet he did not sin" (Hebrews 4:15).

As I invoke the image of the Weeping God, I envision Jesus sitting on his throne in heaven. He knows what I'm going through, and tears slide down his cheeks. Then I "know" the Weeping God feels my pain.

> This High Priest of ours understands our weaknesses, for he faced all of the same testings we do, yet he did not sin (Hebrews 4:15).

⚜ ⚜ ⚜

Jesus, my Weeping God,
you care.
When I hurt, you not only understand my pain,
but you feel it.
When I cry, your tears match mine.
Thank you, Lord Jesus Christ, for being the
Divinely Human One. Amen.

Chapter Forty-Three
The Burden-Bearer

"Praise be to the Lord, to God our Savior, who daily bears our burdens." I like that translation of Psalm 68:19 in the New International Version (NIV), which varies remarkably from the King James Version (KJV). The KJV (or Authorized Version of 1611) translates part of the verse as referring to God "who daily loadeth us with *benefits*."

My research, coupled with my nearly forgotten Hebrew, assures me that the literal translation refers to God as the one who "loads up for us." The idea is that of donkeys or other beasts of burden loaded with provisions. As I read the NIV, I think of God as our Burden-Bearer.

That immediately brings to mind the matter of sin. Almost anyone in the Church can talk about Jesus *bearing* our sins on the cross. It's certainly that—but I think it's more.

I think of Jesus' words in Matthew 11:28–30: "Come to me, all of you who are weary and carry heavy burdens, and I will give you rest. Take my yoke upon you. Let me teach you, because I am humble and gentle at heart, and you will find rest for your souls. For my yoke is easy to bear, and the burden I give you is light."

Jesus spoke to people who desperately wanted to find God, perhaps who wanted to be good, even perfect.

I've translated Jesus' first words above as, "Come to me whoever is exhausted." The plea is for those of us who have tried hard and long to be the good people of God. He recognizes that we're carrying a heavy load as we try to climb upward. If we're not careful, we get entangled with rules and commandments that get mixed up with a kind of cultural Christianity that burdens us and keeps us low.

In Jesus' days, the Jews used the yoke as a symbol of submission. This verse tells us that if we take Jesus Christ's yoke, it fits us well; it doesn't become a heavy-duty, law-upon-law obligation. It's a way of saying he'll help us carry our burdens.

I like that thought. When the people read Psalm 68, they must have thought of their donkeys that carried heavy loads for them. And if they did, what kind of picture did that give them of God, the All-Powerful One?

As I read the psalm centuries later, it gives me hope. It helps me understand how God relates to us.

For instance, I think about Sam, a long-time friend that I care about deeply. More than nine years ago, his son left home after a violent argument. For nine years, Sam had no contact with his son.

Whenever I asked, Sam would shake his head and say, "I don't know where he is or what he's doing." The pain showed on his face.

In April 1996, the son called. "Daddy, can I come and see you?" He was calling from a phone booth two minutes away. It was a tearful reunion, and the breach began to mend. Father's Day was one of the happiest days of Sam's life because his son came to spend the day, along with the rest of the family.

"Nobody will ever know the burden of what I went through for nine years," Sam said. "I cried and cried until no more tears came."

As I listened, I teared up as well. Then Sam said, "If it hadn't been for God, I don't know how I could have held up."

In that instant, I got it: God, the Burden-Bearer. God didn't take away the problem—at least not for nine years. No outward change, no thundering voice in the storm that promised answers. Sam had nothing to go on except the assurance that God cared.

In such situations, we realize we're following the Burden-Bearer of our lives. Today, I sat for a long time meditating on that concept. It gave me comfort to know that God not only understands our pains and hurts, but God intervenes.

Because God has done that, I'm learning not to carry around a lot of worry: that I've failed to live up to my potential; that my pastor (or insert a favorite name here) doesn't understand me; or, that I messed up a month ago by (fill in your own ending).

God doesn't always make things right, not even in nine years—at least not the way we want them to be. Some things in life never have a happy resolution. That's all the more reason we need our Burden-Bearer, who makes life's loads tolerable.

For instance, I once had a friend named Ben—a really close friend—and we had a serious rift between us. It doesn't matter who was right and who was wrong; it was simply that our viewpoints were totally different. He couldn't cross over into my way of thinking, and I couldn't go over to his.

For several days, I prayed for a reconciliation. It didn't come about. That was four years ago. It may never happen. I wrote to Ben, asking him to forgive me. He never replied. Despite the sadness of a broken relationship, God has taken the burden off my back. I have no mind-reading talents, so I don't know how he feels; I know only that he has not replied. But I've been able to let it go: God has been my Burden-Bearer.

Today, I recalled an artist's illustration I'd seen in a long-ago edition of John Bunyon's classic allegory, *Pilgrim's Progress*. The hero, Christian, is heading toward the Celestial City, but he has a heavy burden strapped to his back. Evangelist talks to him, but the burden remains. Finally, as he nears the cross, the burden falls from his back and rolls away. It's Christian's conversion experience, but I see it as an ongoing picture for me and many others.

Unfortunately, most of us get rid of the burdens and then take on new ones. Sometimes we stuff them inside, and deny even to ourselves that they exist.

The kind of burden doesn't matter. He is *the* Burden-Bearer, who's waiting for us to offer our heavy, exhausting loads to him.

> Praise the Lord, praise God our Savior! For each day he carries us in his arms (Psalm 68:19).

God, my Burden-Bearer,
take the load from me.
I'm too weary trying to do it all myself,
attempting to make everything come out perfect,
and I'm tired of failing in my attempts.
Take my burdens and fill me with
your peace and joy. Amen.

Chapter Forty-Four
The Crafter

"Then you're criticizin' God. Right?" Woody Jolly asked.

His words shocked me so much I blurted out, "Maybe you heard something different from what I said."

He laughed and thumped me on the back. "Oh, no, I hear you just fine. For the past quarter hour you've been groanin' and moanin' about what a rotten Christian you are. Right?"

I nodded. Woody reached into his pocket and pulled out his New Testament. I stared at my friend, a soft-spoken man with limited formal education, but one of the most spiritually insightful people I've ever known.

"Just read this," he said, and thrust the New Testament at me.

"For we are God's masterpiece. He has created us anew in Christ Jesus, so we can do the good things he planned for us long ago" (Ephesians 2:10). Some of the older translations refer to us as "his workmanship."

"When you get down hard on yourself and start thinkin' how bad you are, you're criticizin' God, you know." He wasn't joking. "You're a sinner, but you're still God's masterpiece, see?"

"Yes, I see," I said. "It's just the spiritual uplift I need."

That happened fifteen years ago, but I've remembered the words of Ephesians from time to time when my thoughts focused on my failures and shortcomings, and especially after I've blown it in a situation.

Woody had hold of something that I grasped that day. I *am* the work of God.

Here's the context of that verse Woody showed me. The apostle Paul writes: "God saved you by his grace when you believed. And you can't take credit for this; it is a gift from God. Salvation is not a reward for the good things we have done, so none of us can boast about it. For we are God's masterpiece" (Ephesians 2:8–10).

That's rather clear. Our relationship to God is an unearned gift. "When God started on me, he began with inferior material," I said once. Yet when I look at that passage objectively, my self-degradation doesn't hold up.

"What does it mean for me to be your work?" I asked.

As I prayed, I envisioned God as a master crafter. I used to observe African carvers take a block of wood, chip away with a sharp, but crude-looking tool, and within minutes, an elephant or a lion would come to life.

One time I watched a man for perhaps twenty minutes while I waited for friends. He'd finish a carving, pick up a fresh piece of wood, stare at it, and start chipping away. Although he specialized in elephants, he made a variety of wild animals.

"How do you know what animal to make?" I asked.

My question caught him by surprise. He stared at a new piece of wood and began to chip away. "Ah, yes, I know what you mean," he said at last. "You see, I look at this piece of wood. I feel its texture and study its size, and I ask myself, 'What animal is trapped inside this piece of wood that is trying to get outside?' When I know that, I let it out."

That's about as close as I can get to God working in human lives. God has a plan for the world, for all believers, and for us individually. God knows who we are and by some plan unknown to us, the Master Crafter works with us to bring it out.

Some of us are elephants, others lions, gazelles, cheetahs, and there are even a few monkeys among us. My problem is that I don't understand Christians who are gazelles, because I'm an elephant. They don't behave the way I do or think the way I do. (Of course, it also works the other way,)

Ephesians 2:10 also reminds me that I'm only one creation of God. All around me are other examples of God's handiwork. And when I criticize them, I'm criticizing God.

I pondered Paul's strong words to the Romans: "Accept other believers who are weak in faith, and don't argue with them about what they think is right or wrong. For instance, one person believes it's all right to eat anything.... Who are you to condemn someone else's servants? Their own master will judge whether they stand or fall. And with the Lord's help, they will stand and receive his approval" (Romans 14:1–2, 4).

Most of us wouldn't use the word condemn, but we would criticize. The principle is the same. Whenever I criticize a sister or brother, I'm criticizing God. That hurts. That doesn't settle all the problems of human relationships, but it reminds me of the basic fact that I'm a product of divine creation. So are others.

This week, I've been praying for God to help me accept myself as an example of divine crafting at its best. I don't want to complain because I'm not as perfect as I would like to be. *I'm God's work.* That's a powerful statement for me to make—powerful because it means that when I grumble about myself, I deserve a loving rebuke. I am what God has made me. I'm part of a divine product made by a divine crafter of human goods—an example of God's living work.

Today, I thought of several people that I don't agree with and have been critical of. As I prayed, I asked God to help me love the giraffes, monkeys, and cheetahs of my world. I want God to help me celebrate their uniqueness wrought at the hand of the Divine Crafter.

⚜ ⚜ ⚜

For God is working in you, giving you
the desire and the power to do what
pleases him (Philippians 2:13).

Great Crafter,
forgive me for seeing only imperfection in myself
and for seeing it in others.
Like them, I am your work—
lovingly,
carefully,
divinely created by you.
Thank you, Great Crafter, and teach me to rejoice in
all your creation. Amen.

Chapter Forty-Five
The Potter

"Why am I this way? Why can't I change?"

Most of us have heard that cry from troubled individuals. The first time I heard it, it came from a man who had been an alcoholic for almost a decade. He kept trying to quit; once he stayed sober for eight months, and another time for nearly a year. He always went back to the bottle.

I didn't have an answer for him. I don't think he actually asked for an answer. Even if he had received one, it wouldn't have solved his problem.

All of us are less than perfect, and we know it. Probably most of us have things in our personality we've tried to change but have been unsuccessful. We may have mellowed slightly or made some adjustment, but in other areas we just don't seem to win.

Our tendency is to blame God or some other outside force that we're the way we are. Perhaps we were born that way, or our early environment made us that way. How can we change?

When we cry out to God, "Why am I this way?" I wonder if we're asking for information or subtly blaming God for making us the way we are.

We're not the first to question God. Jeremiah, an Old Testament prophet, struggled with this issue when he wrote about watching a potter at work. "So I did as he told me and found the potter working at his wheel. But the jar he was making did not turn out as he had hoped, so he crushed it into a lump of clay again and started over. Then the LORD gave me this message: 'O Israel, can I not do to you as this potter has done to his clay? As the clay is in the potter's hand, so are you in my hand'" (Jeremiah 18:3–6).

God's sovereignty over us is difficult for us to accept. We want free will, power of choice, and the ability to make decisions in our lives.

I don't know where the line falls between God's sovereignty and our ability to change. But we need to remember that we belong to God and are divine possessions; God created us to be who we are.

What would it be like, I asked God, if I accepted myself as I am, without reservation? What would it be like if I took the very position Jeremiah stresses? If God is the potter, and I am clay in the divine hands, who am I to complain, or debate about it? But to acknowledge the full sovereignty of God gives us problems. We just can't quite accept that we have no rights.

I thought of what it would feel like to be a young child, feeling hungry, and waiting for food. Would I sit complacently and say, "Oh, I'll get fed," or would I surge forward, push myself to the table, and scream, "Me, me, me"? Probably the latter.

Part of it, I suppose, has to do with trust or maybe with how many times we have gone hungry. We're simply afraid to turn everything over to God. If we fully surrender, what will God do with us? Where will God take us?

I think of the old hymn sung in countless churches even today: "Thou are the potter, I am the clay. Make me and mold me after thy will, while I am waiting, yielded and still" ("Have Thine Own Way, Lord," 1902).

I've sung those words, and I've meant them. They're a vow—a promise to God and to myself of total commitment.

I'm quick to make that vow until something happens in my life that I don't like. When I'm treated unfairly or unkindly, I'm a first-class complainer.

If we submit to the total sovereignty of God, we're saying, "It doesn't matter what happens in my life, it's okay. You have the right to do anything you want with me." That's not easy for most of us.

For instance, when I receive business opportunities, I ask God to make each of them happen "if it's your will." How should I react when the answer comes? Typically, if I get a yes, I'm joyful and if it's a no, I feel dejected. But I'm not satisfied with that response.

I think of Job who suffered far more trauma than I could imagine happening to me. His wife urged him, "Curse God and die."

Here's his response: "You talk like a foolish woman. Should we accept only good things from the hand of God and never anything bad? ..." (2:10).

That's the attitude I want to have. It's actually a freeing attitude. It's leaving the results in God's hands. They're there anyway, but being a pride-filled human being, that's not easy for me to live with.

When bad things happen to good people—and I'm good people—I don't handle it very well. I don't turn my back on God or deny the faith. No, I pout and moan and tell God, "That's not fair." Then after I've groaned and moaned awhile, I finally hear myself say, "Okay, I'm yours. Whatever you want." It's an eventual surrender.

I want that "eventual surrender" to be an immediate, spontaneous reaction: "I accept your will." As difficult as that is for me, that's how I'm praying.

It's the way Jesus prayed in the garden. "Not my will, but thine be done." I don't think we pray those words unless they're preceded by a deep yearning for something that we think God isn't going to let us have. It may be a marriage partner, a special job, or a sale that will net us a fortune. We pray such a prayer after we tell God what we want, mean it with intensity, and then have it fall apart in front of us.

At such moments, we realize we are clay. The Master Potter shapes and forms us, keeps us on the wheel, trims away the excess, forms us into the vessel that pleases the Potter's experienced eye.

In the midst of that comes the pain and the natural tendency to say, "I'm only human, and I don't like this."

The Master Potter ignores our dissatisfaction and just keeps on working, shaping and reforming, doing what only the Potter does well.

> How foolish can you be? He is the Potter, and he is certainly greater than you, the clay! (Isaiah 29:16).

Great Potter,
forgive me for complaining,
grumbling,
rebelling,
and help me submit to whatever you need to do
to make me into a vessel
that meets your approval. Amen.

Chapter Forty-Six
The Divine Refuge

I marvel at the images the psalmist used to convey his relationship with God. One of those images depicts God as a refuge.

Thinking of God as a refuge conjures certain pictures in my mind. I can see myself running into a cave for protection. Or I think of a sanctuary, which brings to mind a medieval cathedral enclosure, a place of safety. In that era, churches were more than just a place of worship. People came there for sanctuary, begging, "Help me. My life is in danger."

I asked my wife Shirley what "refuge" meant to her. At first, she thought of being safe on a large rock with violent waves below her. Then she said, "I also think of refuge as the wings of a mother hen— the place where baby chicks run when frightened or in danger."

Members of my Sunday school class added: a place of peace, an escape, a place to hide, a place to turn when troubled, protection, security, contentment, a place to get away so you can get yourself together, being away from voice-mail, phones ringing, and demands for your time.

Refuge is a powerful word. It speaks to us of a place that's safe and where we'll find peace. The danger may be nothing more than being the object of gossip, the personal ire of a coworker, facing the loss of a job, or an illness.

These may not seem momentous to an outsider. It's not the events themselves that make them dangerous, but our responses to them. If people gossip against us and it tears us up emotionally, that's serious. Others may shrug or laugh and say, "Consider where it originated." But even petty gossip spread about us can make us want to retreat from our normal way of life, to seek safety, to seek a place where we're understood, loved, and cared for.

Ideally, that's the Church—that is, the people of God. The Church represents refuge for us as we retreat from overwhelming odds and threatening defeats. At its best, the Church wraps its arms around us, soothes us, and tends our wounds until we're ready to return to battle again. When we return to the world again, we're strengthened because we know we have God, as well as human allies, at our side.

Of course, I could easily point out where the Church has failed—and all of us know that only too well. We know it because we're part of the Church. If we're honest with ourselves, we sense that we've failed all too often. In fact, many of us tend to concentrate on the downside, especially when the people of God haven't provided the refuge we crave.

Yet the Church hasn't always failed. Why not look at those times when the Church has provided refuge? Those moments when God's people have embraced the pain-ridden, the guilt-laden, the discouraged, and the grieving?

I recall an African who walked more than seventy miles to come to a convention because someone told him, "God is in that place." He came and found his refuge there.

I think of George, who lost his wife through divorce, his job as a pastor through being fired by the deacons, and his friends by not living the "committed Christian life." (If he had lived a committed life, they reasoned, his wife wouldn't have left him and the deacons wouldn't have fired him.)

One day, a downtrodden George came to our church. Susie and Skip Cothran welcomed him and asked him to sit with them. After the service, they introduced him to their friends.

"I didn't think anyone would love me," George said later, "not if they really knew me." Over a period of three or four months, George found refuge in the church. Then strengthened and spiritually fortified, he took a job and had to move away.

George wrote a letter in which he said, "I was the frog and you people kissed me and turned me into a prince."

George had found sanctuary.

But the secret is not just finding refuge in God's people, but refuge in God. The best we can do is point to the Great Refuge. People hold us, encourage us, love us, but none of those actions or attitudes can provide permanent refuge. When we're tired of fighting, when we've battled our own problems and we wail, "Help me, God, I'm exhausted, I can't make it anymore," we need the Divine Refuge.

I recall a time when I felt so low that I didn't think I'd ever pass out of the valley of the shadow of death. I knew I'd survive physically, but I was at my spiritual end. Because I'm primarily a visual person, as I prayed, I saw myself lying before a stone wall. I saw a door, but it was locked. I cried for help, but no one came. I was ready to give up. Then the door opened, but I felt too exhausted to move. Someone picked me up and carried me inside.

In essence, I had faced a spiritual crisis. Finally, I surrendered to God, and when that happened, the door of God's refuge opened to me. The Divine Refuge carried me inside where I could lie quietly and have my wounds cared for. Then it was as if the voice said, "Be strong. Be of good cheer. I am with you always."

Then I was ready to leave the place of refuge.

I left, but I knew its location. I could always return.

That's what makes the Divine Refuge so meaningful. It's not a place to live. It's not a lifelong escape from the world or the troubles of humanity. It's a temporary place to receive peace, to feel safe, and to be strengthened until we have been fortified inwardly. Then we go out again.

We don't have to go down into the treacherous waves or shoot the rapids. When we leave our place of refuge, we have a new direction. "Your word is a lamp to guide my feet and a light for my path," reads Psalm 119:105.

So even when we are away from the refuge, the Word of God, the presence of divine love, and the fellowship of other believers remind us that the victory is ours.

> My victory and honor come from God alone. He is my refuge, a rock where no enemy can reach me. O my people, trust in him at all times (Psalm 62:7–8).

God of Refuge, God of Sanctuary,
some days I feel totally alone:
Abandoned.
Forsaken.
Defeated.
That's when I run to you.
You are there to protect me from the
onslaught of my enemies,
as well as the hurts from my friends.
God, thank you for giving me refuge
in all my times of trouble.
Amen.

Chapter Forty-Seven
The High Rock

Today is Thursday, and it's been a hard week. Several disappointments have left me pounded and battered from all sides.

I feel like the small raft I had seen once amid the pounding waves and huge rocks in Bermuda. A heavy wave dashed it against a jutting rock. Once the water receded, the wooden raft went back. Several gashes marked the roughness of its beatings. Seconds later came another pounding. I wondered if anyone would come and rescue the raft from the unrelenting forces of nature.

By contrast, the rocks must have been there for centuries. No matter how strong the waves, the rocks never flinched.

I watched as the tide increased the power and frequency of the waves. Later, the tide changed and the depleted force of nature slinked away from the shoreline. But the firm rocks never moved.

I thought of that scene and felt my own disappointments this week, and my mind focused on God our rock. That term appears frequently in the Old Testament, especially in the Psalms. It's one of those words I usually read and skip over. From the recesses of my mind came the words from the KJV: "Lead me to the Rock that is higher than I." It occurs in Psalm 61:2.

As I turned to Psalm 61 and read the entire prayer of eight verses, I realized it's a prayer for security. I think the psalmist is crying, "Lead me to the rock of safety because it's too high for me to climb in my own strength." (The Septuagint, the translation of the Old Testament into Greek, reads: "Set me high on a rock and make me secure.")

The High Rock began to make sense to me, and I envisioned myself being that little raft and grasping for a hold each time a wave thrust me against the craggy boulders. I'd never get up to safety without someone to help me.

As I meditated on that image, I thought of Stone Mountain just outside Atlanta. I live about ten miles from that giant mile-high monolith of granite that protrudes out of nowhere. I've climbed it many times. On the trail, I've seen initials and dates carved on the rock, some that go back forty years, now barely readable. But the rock has stood firm for centuries.

When I thought of God as my High Rock, I prayed, "God, you are my High Rock. You're the strength I need today. You're the force that stands no matter how severe the blows I encounter."

In quiet silence, peace slowly covered me. The problems of the week remained. Within a couple of hours, I'd have to face them again. But I knew I was secure in the Rock that holds me firm.

This image reminds me of the opening of Psalm 40: "I waited patiently for the Lord; he turned to me and heard my cry. He lifted me out of the slimy pit, out of the mud and mire; he set my feet on a rock and gave me a firm place to stand" (Psalm 40:1–2, NIV).

It goes on to give the result of that action: "He put a new song in my mouth, a hymn of praise to our God. Many will see and fear and put their trust in the Lord" (v. 3). This morning those images gave me peace. Like the psalmist, I felt ready to tell the world of God's love that held me secure. I actually felt a joyous song bubbling inside.

Outwardly, nothing had changed. But inwardly, I was safe. The High Rock had lifted me from the battering waves and brought me to safety.

"I don't know how any of this is going to work out," I said to God, "but it doesn't matter as much as it did a little earlier. I'm here with you. That's what really matters. You're my High, Solid Rock."

> I wait quietly before God, for my victory comes from him. He alone is my rock and my salvation, my fortress where I will never be shaken (Psalm 62:1–2).

I love you, Lord; you are my strength. The Lord is my rock, my fortress, and my Savior; my God is my rock, in whom I find protection. He is my shield, the power that saves me, and my place of safety (Psalm 18:1–2).

Hear my cry, O God; attend to my prayer. From the ends of the earth I call to you, I call as my heart grows faint; lead me to the rock that is higher than I. For you have been a refuge, a strong tower against the foe" (Psalm 61:1–3, NIV).

My High Rock,
the forces of life push against me.
I hurt. I feel desolate and alone.
Then I remember. You are the High Rock.
Help me, because I'm too weak and discouraged
to help myself.
And because you are my High Rock,
I know you're going to lift me up. Amen.

Chapter Forty-Eight
The Divine Discipliner

I grew up in a time when most parents spanked their kids. Some of the spankings my dad gave me probably would be labeled as physical abuse today. A strict disciplinarian in many ways, Dad demanded the same behavior from us all. It worked on me. It didn't work on everyone in our family.

Dad thought he was dong the right thing. His methods seemed harsh then; now that I'm grown they still do. I wish he had been a kinder, more gentle soul. Sometimes I felt his beatings were more to vent his own rage than they were to correct me.

Although I don't agree with my father's methods, I must conclude that, whether we like it or not, we *need* discipline. All of us do, and we need other authority figures besides parents to teach right and wrong and enforce these views. We need neighbors and teachers to nod approval or shake their heads when we go contrary to commonly accepted values.

If we grasp this need, we can understand God the Holy Chastiser. How we view this aspect of God depends, I suppose, on our childhood. My tendency in the beginning of my Christian experience was to see God as the Big Whipper, who pounced on me for the slightest infraction. As I learned more about God, I began to see the kinder side.

Still, the Holy Chastiser has been part of my growing experience. When God disciplines me, I can resent it (and I have!); I can rebel (guilty again!); or I can say, "Thanks, God, I needed that" (I'm learning).

In Hebrews chapter twelve, the writer brings out the concept of the Divine Discipliner by using human examples. His readers were those undergoing persecution and hardship, and (surprise!) they didn't like it. He writes: "Think of all the hostility he endured from sinful people; then you won't become weary and give up. After all, you have not yet given your lives in your struggle against sin. And have you forgotten the encouraging words God spoke to you as his children? He said, 'My child, don't make light of the LORD's discipline, and don't give up when he corrects you. For the LORD disciplines those he loves, and he punishes each one he accepts as his child'" (Hebrews 12:3–6).

There we have it. God corrects us for *our good.* In theory, we know that true disciplining is an act of love. Hebrews says children learn by correction, even if the parents are imperfect in their knowledge and wisdom.

I'm a parent and I've been a child, so I can view this from two perspectives. When I functioned at my best, I disciplined my children because I had the maturity to see the consequences of their actions. I recall the time when my then-three-year-old daughter C-C and I stayed overnight with some friends. When we got into the car the next morning, I realized that she had taken a banana. "Did you ask for that?"

She shook her head.

"Honey, that was wrong. We call that sin when we do things we know are wrong." I took C-C back inside and explained.

"Why, that's horrible," the wife said. "You can't call a young child a sinner. She doesn't know what it means."

"She's learning," I said, not wanting to make a major crime out of her action. But she had stolen, and as her father, I wanted her to be aware of her actions and the consequences of her deed.

Looking back, I may have induced more guilt than my children needed, and sometimes I acted arbitrarily. I may have become too concerned over trivial things and ignored weightier issues. My only response is that I acted with the best wisdom I had.

That's what separates our ways from God's. We're not perfect. As children, we may resent the actions or inconsistencies of our parents. Yet once we become parents, we understand a little more of God's discipline in our lives.

The Divine Discipliner nudges, urges, and even punishes us—whatever it takes—to move us along the road of obedience. "And we know that God causes everything to work together for the good of those who love God and are called according to his purpose for them. For God knew his people in advance, and he chose them to become like his Son, so that his Son would be the firstborn among many brothers and sisters" (Romans 8:28–29). That's God's ultimate purpose at work in us.

Yet when God slaps my fingers, I usually don't see that as part of the divine plan for my life. Sometimes I don't think I did anything wrong and can't see the long-term effects of God's actions or purpose.

One of the things I've learned about the Divine Discipliner came when I overheard a father and his little boy when they visited us. The child wanted his father to do something for him and his dad said no. The son demanded loudly. The father got down on his haunches until he was at eye level. "I love you, Robbie. That's why I said no." He put one arm around the boy and held him while he used his other arm to take out his handkerchief and wipe away the child's tears.

That was one of the best examples of parenting I've ever seen. Maybe the verses in Hebrews chapter twelve are meant to say essentially the same thing to us. "I'm doing this because I love you," God is saying. "Even if you don't understand or don't agree, please trust me that it's for your good."

I'm getting the message, but then I wonder how I should pray to the Divine Discipliner. I'm not crazy enough to ask for God to make things tough for me. Yet I do want to be as much like Jesus Christ as it's possible for me to become.

That means accepting holy correction when it comes. In my praying to the Divine Discipliner, I've asked, "God, make me everything you want me to be and do whatever it takes to make me conform." I ask the Divine Discipliner to show me how to make the right decisions, to do the things that honor God and lead to having God's ultimate purpose fulfilled in me.

On occasion, I've felt like the boy whose parent has just denied him something he's wanted badly. It hurts—really hurts—to face disappointments, to work hard and have it fall apart, to throw myself into something and have a coworker get the promotion or credit instead of me.

I have to remind myself that God's arm is around my shoulder, that the Loving Discipliner is wiping away my tears. In those moments of pain and self-pity, I keep reminding myself, God loves me. God is doing this to make me more like Jesus.

That doesn't take away the pain, but it does help me realize that God truly cares. It gives me a spiritual boost when I think that God slapped my wrist out of love. God's discipline in my life assures me that God has accepted me and won't allow me to settle for less than the divine, ultimate plan for my life.

At times, I've resisted, like Peter did at the Last Supper when Jesus wanted to wash his feet. He refused, but Jesus told him that if he didn't submit he wouldn't have any part of him. So Peter said, "Then don't stop with just my feet. Wash my whole body."

That's what I pray for—total discipline by the divine hand. I still don't like it; it hurts when God tells me no. Yet I choose to rejoice every time the Divine Discipliner works in me.

Discipline me, O God, discipline me.

> For our earthly fathers disciplined us for a few years, doing the best they knew how. But God's discipline is always good for us, so that we might share in his holiness. No discipline is enjoyable while it is happening—it's painful! But afterward there will be a peaceful harvest of right living for those who are trained in this way (Hebrews 12:10–11).

> My child, don't reject the LORD's discipline, and don't be upset when he corrects you. For the LORD corrects those he loves, just as a father corrects a child in whom he delights (Proverbs 3:11–12).

Cecil Murphey

Divine Discipliner,
when you punish me
I moan and wail,
I question your love and your actions.
Forgive me,
and help me understand you are manifesting
your parental love for me.
Remind me of that again and again
until the time comes when I can say in the
midst of disappointments,
"Thanks, God, for loving me enough to stop me." Amen.

Chapter Forty-Nine
The Lifter of My Head

Depression isn't a word I ordinarily associate with myself. It's touched me occasionally, but only three or four times in my life have I fallen to a low, low spot. When I'm down, my body shows it. For example, I hang my head, unable to look up.

When I hang my head it reflects my state of mind—shame, depression, despair, or uncertainty.

This makes me think of King David when Absalom, his son, usurps the throne. Instead of staying and fighting, the elderly monarch and a few trusted friends leave Jerusalem on foot. "David walked up the road to the Mount of Olives, weeping as he went. His head was covered and his feet were bare as a sign of mourning. And the people who were with him covered their heads and wept as they climbed the hill" (2 Samuel 15:30).

That may sound a little more extreme than the way we would respond today. They acted out what they felt.

If we are to believe the titles under the psalm, which are not part of the original text, Psalm 3 tells the poetic version of David's flight from his own son. It calls for deliverance, but in the middle of it, David makes a striking statement: "But you, O Lord, are a shield around me, my glory, the One who lifts my head high" (3:3).

In thinking of that psalm, I particularly meditate on the phrase, "the One who lifts my head high." It presents a beautiful image for us. It's as if we are kneeling before a king, our heads lowered, perhaps even fearful, supplicants prostrate before the throne. We're facing the one who has the power of life and death by his word. The king reaches down, clasps our chins and with his own hands lifts our face upward. Now we look directly into his face. That gesture is to show that we have found favor with the ruler. The literal translation is to "make high" the head.

In the Bible, it's intriguing to see ways in which the idea of the position of the head is used. For instance, Nehemiah tells of the rebuilding of Jerusalem after the exile in Babylon. When Sanballat and others try to stop their work, the writer cries out, "Hear us, our God, for we are being mocked. May their scoffing fall back on their own heads ..." (Nehemiah 4:4). Psalm 7:16 reads, "The trouble they make for others backfires on them. The violence they plan falls on their own heads."

Or, "For he will conceal me there when troubles come; he will hide me in his sanctuary. He will place me out of reach on a high rock. Then I will hold my head high above my enemies who surround me" (Psalm 27:5–6).

Here's a nice contrast: "O Sovereign LORD, my strong deliverer, you shield my head in the day of battle. Do not grant the wicked their desires, LORD" (Psalm 140:7–8 NIV).

The best image of the lifting up of the head comes from an incident recorded in the story of Nehemiah, the cup bearer of King Artaxerxes of Persia. He writes: "Early the following spring, in the month of Nisan, during the twentieth year of King Artaxerxes' reign, I was serving the king his wine. I had never before appeared sad in his presence. So the king asked me, 'Why are you looking so sad? You don't look sick to me. You must be deeply troubled.' Then I was terrified, but I replied, 'Long live the king! How can I not be sad?" (Nehemiah 2:1–3).

Nehemiah tells the king about his sadness for the destroyed city of Jerusalem. The king lifts Nehemiah's head by listening to his servant and granting him permission and provision to rebuild Jerusalem.

This is the lifting up of the head—something all of us need at times. I can think of a couple of times when I've said harsh words, done something stupid, or behaved badly. I felt so guilty and ashamed of my actions that I couldn't look anyone in the eye. I kept my head down and my eyes averted.

The other day I pulled out in front of another driver. I honestly didn't see him, but that didn't excuse me. He leaned on his horn and swerved around me. I held my head low and avoided his gaze. I knew I was wrong.

Isn't that the way we are with God? Awareness of failure makes us drop our gaze, or even avoid praying.

Here's another example. In an irritated mood, I had said several harsh things to a man that calls me three or four times a week and wants to chat for half an hour. During a morning run the next day as I ran down the quiet street, I kept thinking of what I had said to the man. Even though I had apologized immediately, I felt ashamed. It was as if I couldn't look God in the eyes as I prayed. I raced along the road, my eyes on the ground in front of me.

"I'm sorry," I kept saying. "I've hurt someone and I know that pierces your heart too. Forgive me."

I kept running, my heart heavy, and my steps seemed too slow. I probably told God a dozen times I was sorry. Then I felt a wave of peace come over me. It was as if God lifted my chin so that I could look into divine eyes, and then said, "I forgive you."

I didn't hear words. I didn't need to.

I knew that God had lifted my head and shown me favor.

> Why am I discouraged? Why is my heart so sad? I will put my hope in God! I will praise him again—my Savior and my God! (Psalm 42:110).

But You, O LORD, are a shield around me; you are my glory, the one who holds my head high. I cried out to the LORD, and he answered me from his holy mountain (Psalm 3:3–4).

Lifter of My Head,
thank you for making me look upward,
and thank you for looking down on me with favor.
May I ever be faithful to you. Amen.

Chapter Fifty
The Gifter

"I have a gift of writing," he said as he thrust his manuscript at me.

"Oh, uh, that's, uh, fine," I said. His words shocked me; I had never heard anyone talk that way before.

I took the proffered pages, trying to think of an appropriate response without calling him crazy. To my amazement, when I read his material, the article flowed. By the third paragraph, I had forgotten his words and my eyes moved on.

"This is good," I said, "and you won't have any problem getting this published." Of course, I saw "a few places" where he could polish and tighten.

He thanked me for the encouragement and moved on. This happened at a writers conference in 1989. I don't remember his name or very much about the manuscript. But I couldn't forget his words.

He had a gift; he knew he had a gift; he wasn't reticent to acknowledge it. He didn't seek my confirmation of his ability—that's probably what affected me most. He spoke with an inner assurance that didn't need my approving response.

I admire people who can talk that way and mean it. They know what they can do, and they easily acknowledge it's a *gift*, not some earned possession or reward for studying hard.

When I talk about gifts—especially what I label as spiritual gifts—I believe they come from outside ourselves. We simply have them and we can't explain why or how they came to us. We usually need training to polish those talents, but they're there. They're a part of ourselves like our speech patterns or the way we hold a pencil.

The apostle Paul writes that we all have gifts. It's important to say that because some tend to say, "Oh, well, God forgot about me," or "I have no gifts." Gifts may not be developed, or they may be the less flashy kinds, but the Bible says *all* of us have them.

The apostle writes, "There are different kinds of spiritual gifts, but the same Spirit is the source of them all. There are different kinds of service, but we serve the same Lord. God works in different ways, but it is the same God who does the work in all of us. A spiritual gift is given to each of us so we can help each other" (1 Corinthians 12:4–7).

I want to tell you about a woman with a gift. Shortly after I started to publish, Marion Bond West joined our editing group, the Scribe Tribe. My wife read Marion's first submission and said, "She can't spell, she can't punctuate, she doesn't know the meaning of grammar, but she sure can write." Shirley spotted the gift, unpolished as it was. (Since then Marion has published seven books and has the distinction of being *Guideposts'* most published author.) The editors agree: She sure can write. Marion has a gift.

When I talk about gifts, I don't think of the condensed menu in the New Testament, such as Paul lists in 1 Corinthians 12 and 14. When I think of giftedness, I refer to those talents that are simply in our lives without our struggling to attain them.

I think of my father who had the ultimate green thumb. He could stick anything in the ground and it rooted itself. He developed a number of varieties of tomatoes, long before hybrid brands came out.

Years ago, Miriam White was the pianist at a church where Shirley and I worshiped for 14 years. When she played the offertory or postlude, I felt something emanating from that grand piano. It was her gift, and she also developed it.

Years ago, I talked with Esther, a secretary at a Bible college, whose father and brothers were all preachers and teachers. "Are you thinking of following in the family footsteps?" I asked.

Esther bent forward and wrapped her arms around her Remington typewriter. "This is my gift and my ministry," she said.

Others come to mind. When the late Arthur Dodzweit was my pastor, he emanated a spirit of caring and compassion. Margie Butts showed the gift of calmness in handling turmoil and tumult. Her presence seemed to calm others. Anne Dunnivan knew how to listen. Her posture, her frequent nods, and especially the aliveness of her eyes told me that she listened to every word.

Gifts from God. We all have them.

Most of us don't feel comfortable in acknowledging them. In our Western culture, it sounds boastful to say, "God has given me the gift to teach" or "God has gifted me to be a baseball player."

Maybe it's time for us to change that. Maybe it's time for us—the ones who know that "all things come from God"—to bring honor to the Giver. Too many of us have exulted in the gift as if we had created it, earned it, developed it, or discovered it totally by self-effort.

Here is part of how I have been praying: "Show me my giftedness. Help me acknowledge these gifts and develop them."

To acknowledge a gift is to acknowledge the Giver. When I lay claim to having a gift, it doesn't mean I'm the best in the world, or that I rank third from the top. It simply means I have a talent—an ability—that God has been pleased to give me.

I have two gifts for which I'm immensely thankful. I can write and I can teach. I don't have to compare my gift to anyone else's. I could name half-a-dozen writers I admire immensely. I don't envy them or feel jealous. (In my thinking, envy means I want what the person has; jealous means I wish they didn't have it.) I can rejoice with their accomplishments. I can read other writers and say,

"This is good stuff." Yet their writing says nothing about mine.

I'm responsible to God for the cultivation of my gifts. They didn't come to me fully developed and trained. The spark of divinely given talent was there; I had to cooperate with God to enhance it.

Isn't it also true that we sometimes serve better if we have gifts we're not aware of? Consider what I call the gifts of kindness and genuine humility. They're more precious in demonstration than when the gifted are aware of them.

But when God does make us aware of talents, that lays responsibility on us. We're going to be held accountable for the things we do as well as the things we don't do. If God makes us aware of a gift of any kind, God wants us to acknowledge it, give thanks for it, and use it. We honor God when we use our spiritually given abilities. Conversely, I believe we deny God when we don't acknowledge and use those gifts.

So I've been praying about my giftedness because I know its purpose is to uplift others. If we have an ability, it's not there to make us feel good, but to be "a special way of serving others." In 1 Corinthians, Paul wrote about spiritual gifts and listed nine of them (see 1 Corinthians 12:8–10). Then he concluded, "It is the one and only Spirit who distributes all these gifts. He alone decides which gift each person should have" (v. 11).

But what about our worthiness? Do we have to be more spiritual first? At one point that question troubled me. Then I realized that a gift is a gift; it's not a matter for boasting, only for accepting. Consider Samson who had a gift of strength. Morally, he was weak, but his spiritual gift and his moral behavior were quite different issues. I thought of a deposed televangelist. I believe he had a gift to heal that often worked; I also think his personal life didn't match his spiritual talent.

Once I was able to get past that issue, I prayed for God to help me to recognize my gifts, enhance them, and use them to help others. And when I help others, I glorify God in the process.

Recently I've become aware of another gift that I've had for a long time. I'm not going to name it, but the recognition was one of those "Aha!" moments. At first it scared me. It felt so awesome, something too big for me. Even so, I thought, I've been praying about my spiritual giftedness. If the Gift Giver is pleased to reveal this to me—and I felt that's what happened—that makes me responsible to do something about it.

Such thoughts make me rejoice. I keep thinking, God has *entrusted* me with this gift. It has pleased God to give this to me, so I need to learn how to be more effective in using it.

> In his grace, God has given us different gifts for doing certain things well.... (Romans 12:6).

CECIL MURPHEY

⚜ ⚜ ⚜

Giver of Good Gifts,
thank you for the gifts you have given me
to glorify you
by enriching my own life
and those of others. Amen.

Chapter Fifty-One
The Introvert

Jesus was an introvert. At least that's my conclusion. Extroverts get their energy and motivation from outside; introverts from within. When I talk with people to find out which they are—and it's not always obvious—I ask them two simple questions.

1. You have the day off, and you're feeling sluggish. Do you close the door and go to bed or call friends on the telephone?
2. You go to a party where there are people you know. After an hour, are you ready to leave or do you get charged up as the evening wears on?

As you may have figured out, extroverts get on the phone and feel charged up from being around a group of people.

I'm an extrovert, and my tendency is to call friends. When I attend parties, I usually stay until they get ready to shut the doors, because my energy gets a boost from being around other people.

As I look at Jesus, it seems rather obvious that he was what I'd call an internal man. He frequently went away from his disciples to what the Bible calls a solitary place. There he prayed.

When the crowds followed him, at night he slipped away so he could be alone. In his famous scene in the Garden of Gethsemane, he took his three closest disciples with him. While they slept, he prayed—just Jesus and God.

Knowing that helps me immensely. During the first twenty years of my Christian experience, I devoured books, articles, and pamphlets about how to live the dedicated Christian life. They usually told me to do something of the Jesus style—solitude, getting away from others, and spending hours and hours alone.

That's the part I always had trouble with: hours alone. Oh, maybe only one or two, but every day? I'm not fussing about it on the basis of the busyness of my life. It has to do with my personality, and I finally figured it out.

Those books, tracts, and articles were written by introverts and sold to us extroverts. Unconsciously, they tried to make us like them. Because they naturally turned inward, they assumed that was the way—the only way—for everybody who wanted to live a godly life.

I confess that although my tree is planted on the extroverted side of the fence, some of my branches lean to the other side. Probably everyone has some leanings the other way, and none of us are purely one type. But no one ever told me that I could be a godly person and not be like the saints of old who wore calluses on their knees from much praying and being alone with God.

Because I didn't know that, guilt constantly nipped at me.

I couldn't make my life function like those introverts such as my friend Kiki, who said, "If God let me choose my life, I would be content to get away from people and live the contemplative life." Terry put it differently by saying, "I don't really need people. I'm able to be by myself and enjoy my own company. Being with other people is like an interruption."

My wife, Shirley, is a classic introvert. She finds deep joy in spending enormous amounts of time alone with God. She can be at home for ten hours and not talk to another soul or turn on the TV or radio, and she feels contented. That's not a picture of me.

I've been working at this for a long time, and I can spend an occasional hour in prayer and say, "Hey, thanks, God, that was nice." Normally a half hour passes and I'm ready for physical movement and something to happen. I've adapted by breaking my prayer times into two portions a day, and that helps.

I've finally come to accept that Jesus is my model—an introvert—but he also loves us extroverts. I expect I'm more like the personality of the apostle Peter. In the Gospels, he seems to do the extroverted things. I like that because Peter was as close to Jesus as any of the others. If not the first head of the church, he was certainly number one of the original apostles. For the first twelve chapters of Acts, the light focuses primarily on him.

Yet for many years I tried to change myself into the introverted type. It didn't work. I tried to take on a personality that wasn't my own. Perhaps part of maturing in the Christian faith is recognizing who we really are and accepting that reality.

This morning as I talked to the Introvert, I believe he understood. As an extrovert, I like the fact that he's a good listener, and that I receive new energy just being around him. He understands that I pray better when I walk. I do my very best praying when I run for an hour before daylight. He understands that I get wearied after trying to pray on my knees for forty-five minutes.

In my prayer time today (and some of it was in a quiet, all-but-motionless position), I was able to rejoice that I'm all right as an extrovert. If Jesus could have a loving relationship with my spiritual mentor, Peter, it's all right for Cec to be an extrovert. Instead of trying to structure my prayer and devotional time to look like that of Shirley or a Trappist monk, I have to learn to be the real me.

I don't want to use my personality type as an excuse not to pray or read my Bible. Instead, I capitalize on the re-energizing I receive being in the presence of another. Instead of phoning two of my friends to lift my spirits, I'm learning to draw on the energy from being in God's presence. I draw on that energy while my body is moving. I'm with Jesus the Introvert. (And I read recently that introverts are especially attracted to extroverts. I like that statement.)

The more aware I am of the presence of God in my life, and the more vivid that presence becomes, the more my extroverted personality flows. And the more I become the real me.

And God loves the real me, no matter who I am.

> Before daybreak the next morning, Jesus got up and went out to an isolated place to pray (Mark 1:35).

Jesus, Perfect Man, Perfect God,
I am who I am, by your grace.
Help me value myself and the kind of personality you've given me.
I'm yours, no matter who I really am.
And you accept me just as I am. Amen.

Chapter Fifty-Two
The Quiet Listener

At least twenty years have passed since I read the novel, *The Listener* by Taylor Caldwell. I remember little of the story line, but a minister talked to troubled people and then sent them into a room. Once inside, where they were alone, they were to open themselves totally and talk to the Listener. No answers came to the speakers except the voices they heard within their own hearts. Yet the people had profound experiences that changed their lives.

The Listener in the quiet room was a metaphor, so far as I could figure out, of the author's concept of prayer. It was a bit simplistic, I thought at the time. Yet, even twenty years later, I still remember that part about going into the silent room and speaking to the Listener.

I've remembered, I suppose, because the idea intrigues me. Few of us grasp the value of listening—total concentrated listening. We may sit in silence, but too often we're pondering our own thoughts or figuring out what to answer.

Sometimes God is that Quiet Listener; he doesn't speak—not a word—and yet somehow we know we've been heard.

And we are confident that he hears us whenever we ask for anything that pleases him. And since we know he hears us when we make our requests, we also know that he will give us what we ask for (1 John 5:14–15).

The eyes of the Lord watch over those who do right, and his ears are open to their prayers (1 Peter 3:12).

What do we learn from these references? God hears us even when we don't feel as if we've gotten through. When God chooses to listen in silence, it doesn't mean pleasure or displeasure. It means only that God hears but doesn't speak. Sometimes the lack of words is more profound than any message. In the quietness, we turn inward, to ponder our own hearts. We search deeply and hear the sounds of the silence.

That may sound like some mystical statement from a New Age groupie or what a sixteenth-century quietist might have said. Despite the possibility of being misinterpreted, I think they were on to something.

Probably most of us want to talk to God without always speaking words. We want to hear God's silence. We know about God listening and answering. That makes prayer meaningful. We speak and know we're heard. Or as the psalmist says, even before we think it, God already knows our thoughts (see Psalm 139:4).

Maybe we should rethink praying to the Quiet Listener. We get filled with telling God things or waiting for God to speak, act, or direct us. We're too busy pumping out requests, praise, and thanks to give God a chance to do much except listen. We seldom pause long enough to experience the Quiet Listener. Is it because we're afraid of the power of silence?

Instead of assuming that silence is disapproval or God turning away from us, maybe it's God's most powerful way of communicating. The Quiet Listener may simply want us to experience the stillness.

That stillness is something like the value of silence between close friends. When I'm with my friend David Morgan, we occasionally sit in silence. It's not because we have nothing to say. In some ways it may be the most articulate of our communication. We're comfortable being with each other. It's a time of peace, and neither has the burden to keep things going. We don't always have to use words or need an agenda. Being together is enough for both of us.

Once in a while I've experienced the Quiet Listener that way. I've come into the holy presence, and didn't need to have anything to pray about. I listened to the silence and enjoyed the moment. I used to say I was basking in the presence of God.

It took me a long time to figure out how meaningful such an experience can be. Experiencing the Quiet Listener may be more profound than many of the times I've heard God's answer.

I open my heart to God, tears flow, and in the silence, there is consolation. It comes from God the Quiet Listener.

> The Lord is good to those who depend on him, to those who search for him. So it is good to wait quietly for salvation from the Lord. And it is good for people to submit at an early age to the yoke of his discipline: Let them sit alone in silence beneath the Lord's demands (Lamentations 3:25–28).

Quiet Listener,
I'm so used to words,
and sometimes I get uncomfortable when I can't
speak or hear words.
Teach me to enjoy your presence,
to value the stillness. Amen.

Chapter Fifty-Three
God's Hidden Face

For nearly eight months I lived with one single biblical passage. Although I read others, almost every day I came back to Lamentations 3. Here are the major verses:

> I am the one who has seen the afflictions that come from the rod of the LORD's anger. He has led me into darkness, shutting out all light. He has besieged and surrounded me with anguish and distress. He has buried me in a dark place, like those long dead. He has walled me in, and I cannot escape. He has bound me in heavy chains. And though I cry and shout, he has shut out my prayers. He has blocked my way with a high stone wall; he has made my road crooked. He has hidden like a bear or a lion, waiting to attack me. He has dragged me

off the path…leaving me helpless and devastated. He has drawn his bow and made me the target for his arrows. He shot his arrows deep into my heart. He has made me chew on gravel. He has rolled me in the dust. Peace has been stripped away, and I have forgotten what prosperity is. I cry out, "My splendor is gone! Everything I had hoped for from the LORD is lost!" The thought of my suffering and homelessness is bitter beyond words. I will never forget this awful time, as I grieve over my loss (Lamentations 3:1–2, 5–13, 16–20).

I wouldn't begin to compare my problems with those of the prophet, but this passage captured my mood: God had let me down.

During those months, I prayed. I scrutinized my life. I searched my past, wondering if I had gone down the wrong road months earlier. Was I deceiving myself in thinking that I was all right with God? If I was all right, then why didn't God answer? Why didn't God smile—just a little?

Nothing but darkness filled my life. I don't mean I was bedridden with depression or heavily medicated. I kept it all inside. It wasn't a faith crisis—the dark night of the soul kind of thing. It was more that God was out there someplace, but not anywhere near me.

Then I began to notice the number of times the Old Testament speaks of God's hidden face.

It seemed not so much that God ran away or hid behind clouds of gloom. It was more the idea that God's face turned away from the people of God.

We know the feeling. Most of us have been snubbed by someone. We approach, extend a hand or smile, only to have the person turn away. We know the person saw us, but we might as well have been invisible or not present.

That's how I felt God treated me.

Day after day, I read Lamentations 3; I found comfort that I had connected with the pain of another person. Yet his words gave me no solution. God's face was still turned away. I prayed, I confessed, I promised, yes, I even bargained, but nothing seemed to work.

Then I lingered on a psalm that has since become a permanently marked place in my Bible: "O LORD, how long will you forget me? Forever? How long will you look the other way? How long must I struggle with anguish in my soul, with sorrow in my heart every day? ... Turn and answer me, O LORD my God! Restore the sparkle to my eyes, or I will die" (Psalm 13:1–3).

"If God would just tell me what I've done wrong or show me where I've gone astray," I wailed to my friend Bob.

"Maybe you haven't gone astray. Maybe God has a different purpose in mind." Bob's what I call a spiritual man, someone who doesn't speak rashly. "Is it possible that this is a time of *waiting* for you and not one of punishment or anger? Do you suppose

God wants to do something in you that can happen only in darkness?"

"What would that be?" I asked.

"Ask God," he said, and smiled.

I asked. I asked. I asked. For days I bombarded heaven with my plea. A few times I got angry. "You want your people to pray, and then you won't listen. Or if you're listening, you're keeping it a secret. What kind of God are you?"

As angry as I got, I somehow knew I could tell God how I felt. I believed God cared and heard me even though nothing happened.

From late September until the middle of summer, God's face stayed turned away from me. I continued to pray, sometimes merely out of ritual or habit. I felt as if my fists had become bloody from beating against a six-inch steel door. But I didn't give up.

Other times I tried to get God to hurry up and respond, but that seemed to throw me backward. Finally, I surrendered. "Okay, God, I'm willing to wait." Every day I heard myself saying things such as, "God, I don't like it, but I'm waiting for you to turn your face toward me again."

My life did change—slowly. In fact, it was so slow and gradual that I was hardly aware of anything being different. But one day, I realized that a sliver of light had crept back into my life. I no longer wept over Psalm 13 or wailed over Lamentations 3. The dawn started to streak across the horizon. It was the beginning of God's face turning toward me again.

At that point, I did a quick checkup on my life. What had happened in the months of darkness? I knew the situation had forced me to pray more—not merely in volume, but in intensity. It had been years since I had burrowed into the Bible as deeply as I did then. As far as I knew, I opened every part of my life to God's searchlight. I didn't always like what I saw, and I asked God's help in making changes.

As more and more light penetrated my dark world, I began thanking God. I could hardly believe it, but I was giving thanks to God for darkness, for uncertainty, for confusion, for pain, for all the difficulties. Yes, I did—because "And we know that God causes everything to work together for the good of those who love God and who are called according to his purpose for them" (Romans 8:28).

Then I realized those days and nights of agony had strengthened me. I don't want to repeat them. And I know Bob was right: God had a different purpose in mind.

> I waited patiently for the LORD to help me, and he turned to me and heard my cry. He lifted me out of the pit of despair, out of the mud and the mire. He set my feet on solid ground and steadied me as I walked along. He has given me a new song to sing, a hymn of praise to our God (Psalm 40:1–3).

Revitalize Your Prayer Life

God, I hate darkness.
I hate the silence.
I hate it when you turn your face from me.
But I've finally learned: it's only for a short time,
and you never leave me.
You're always there—even in the deepest darkness.
Thanks, God. Amen.

Chapter Fifty-Four
The Sender

"You're the only ones I can trust," the old man whispered in his thick accent to the three younger men. "I'm counting on each of you. But even if two of you fail, there is a chance that the third one will make it."

That's a scene from a World War II flick I watched on TV.

The old man was dying, but he had gathered important information the Allied forces needed to defeat the Germans in a significant battle. The film revolved around the three men and the different routes they took. Two of them were caught and killed, but the third, the hero of the film, delivered the important message.

"I was sent, and I couldn't fail." Even though wounded, he handed the officer a coded sheet of paper before he passed out.

The film stirred me to think that those three men dedicated their lives to delivering a message. It made me realize that if we seriously read the commands of the Bible, that's the kind of challenge we have from Jesus Christ.

Jesus sends us; we go. Simple.

In evangelical churches, we don't have to attend very long before we get inundated about witnessing for our faith. In some of them, we even have choices of a half dozen surefire evangelism programs that will bring others to Christ.

Such an approach implies that God intends every single believer to be an evangelist. They try to get around that and simply call us witnesses. I've been in those situations and felt the grips of guilt for not being effective in witnessing. I've done it door-to-door, spoken in public forums, handed out tracts, memorized long lists of presumed objections with scriptural answers. I've done open-air meetings in the United States, Central America, and Africa.

Despite all that, it seems to me that the concept of evangelism as practiced today is too restrictive. We put the entire gospel into one phase—bringing others to the knowledge of Jesus Christ. I don't minimize the importance of evangelism. But when Jesus commissioned his disciples, he had a much broader purpose in mind.

According to John's Gospel, Jesus met with his eleven remaining disciples in the Upper Room after the Resurrection. "Again he said, 'Peace be with you. As the Father has sent me, so I am sending you'" (John 20:21).

Jesus Christ sent the first handful of disciples into the world. Matthew's Gospel ends with what we call the Great Commission and the book of Acts begins with a similar command.

My understanding of Jesus' commission is that he sends us with the total gospel. That is, he sends us to share the good news, but he also sends us to live it. To live it means to behave in such a way that our *lifestyle* attracts others to Jesus Christ.

In another translation, Jesus' words read, "Peace to you! As the Father has sent Me, I also send you" (John 20:21, NKJV). If I get it right, it says that God sent Jesus, now Jesus sends us. It's not a commission to die on the cross—that job's been fulfilled. But the commission is to teach and live the message of God's love.

Here's where I fall short. I can give instructions about coming to Jesus or expound on just about any doctrine of the Bible. The hard part for me is to live the message I proclaim.

As I reflect on the life of Jesus, I realize he taught about God, but he also embodied God's message. He was both the message *and* the messenger.

In another place in this book, I point out that Jesus' disciples came to him one day and asked him to teach them to pray. Why did they do that? Not just because he told them to pray, but because they *observed* him at prayer.

Or think about the scribes and Pharisees who came to him with questions. Some came out of sincere desire to know, others to mock, a few to discredit. The point is, they came. Why did they bother Jesus? I can think of only one reason: he lived what he taught.

Now, two thousand years later, Jesus sends me out into the world with the same commission. For Cec Murphey, it means I'm to go out to my world and live what I have learned, to embody the gospel by my actions as much as by my words.

Here's something else to consider: Jesus' teachings. At the end of the Sermon on the Mount, it says: "When Jesus had finished saying these things, the crowds were amazed at his teaching, for he taught with real authority—quite unlike their teachers of religious law" (Matthew 7:28–29).

I've been feeling great concern over my faithfulness in delivering the message. It's easy to misinterpret, reinterpret, corrupt the intent, overemphasize the parts I like, and under-emphasize the ones I don't.

The church has been doing it for centuries. In some periods, leaders have hit hard on laws and at other times on grace. Twenty years ago, every denomination seemed to have some internal argument over the "charismatic renewal." In the early '90s, how many books did we suddenly see about angels, as if they were the ultimate spiritual experience?

All those things scare me a little. I'm as human as anyone else. I get caught up in trends too. I over-emphasize one phase of the message, which implies an under-emphasis elsewhere.

Yet all the while, I'm responsible to the Sender. When I'm at my best, I hear myself praying, as I did today, "Jesus, help me live the life that honors you."

I sometimes say it in other ways, but my concern is to grasp the message right so that I live it right. If I live it right, I'll share it rightly.

Unfortunately, I never do seem to quite get it right. I can blame it on being a fallible, sinful human being, but I have to keep trying.

I think about two Old Testament stories. God told King Hezekiah that destruction would come to his kingdom, but because he had been a good man, it wouldn't happen during his lifetime. To Hezekiah's grandson, Josiah, came a similar message. The difference in the two stories is the reaction of the two kings.

Hezekiah sighs and says, "Well, at least it won't happen in my time." Josiah goes all out to institute religious reform.

Isn't that how it works with us? When we look at our lives, we see how we've mangled the message (if we're honest with ourselves) by living less-than-perfect lives. Are we like Hezekiah and say, "Oh, well, Jesus, I'm saved"?

Or do we take the Josiah approach and cry out, "Jesus, help me get the message right. Help me teach it right by living it right."

In my praying today, I focused on Jesus the perfect messenger of God. He came to earth and modeled the message. If we examine his life, we began to grasp what God wants of us. Our motivation is to deliver the message pure and untampered with. And if we do it right, people *know* and we don't always have to tell them how spiritual or committed to God we really are.

An example comes to mind of our days in Africa. My wife worked with women and particularly helped them set up Sunday schools and training classes. She slept in the village, ate their food, and walked from village to village—like any African woman.

Only later did she learn that she was the first to "go native." Her predecessor brought her own cot and bedding and demanded boiled water.

When we prepared to move from the area, one of the women came to Shirley. With tears in her eyes, she told my wife how much she had meant to them. The African woman's appreciation sounded critical of Shirley's predecessor.

"Wait," Shirley said, "I know her. She worked hard and ..."

"Yes, that is true," the woman said. "She worked very hard, perhaps harder than you. But she only worked with us. You have loved us, and because you have loved us, we have listened more carefully to you."

Is that what the Sender wants to get across to us? As important as purity of doctrine is or the primacy of evangelism, have we put doctrine or activity or zeal ahead of the real message—the embodiment that Jesus lived before us?

As I examined my own heart today and asked the Sender to help me live the gospel, I thought of the words of Jesus to his disciples just before the

Last Supper: "Dear children, I will be with you only a little longer.... So now I am giving you a new commandment: Love each other. Just as I have loved you, you should love each other. Your love for one another will prove to the world that you are my disciples" (John 13:33a, 34–35).

The Sender wants us to get the message right, and to do so means we've got to embody it by living it. That means a constant self-examination and asking the Sender to help us decontaminate the message.

As we face this, we realize the one thing that will make up for our deficiencies is love. Once people understand that we love them, they allow for our mistakes and shortcomings. That's where we find hope as we ask the Perfect Sender to perfect the message in our lives.

> Jesus came and told his disciples, "I have been given all authority in heaven and on earth. Therefore, go and make disciples of all the nations, ... Teach these new disciples to obey all the commands I have given you. And be sure of this: I am with you always, even to the end of the age" (Matthew 28:18–20).

REVITALIZE YOUR PRAYER LIFE

My Heavenly Sender,
thank you for sending me to represent you.
Forgive me when I present you in a
less-than-perfect manner.
Thank you for trusting me enough to send me out to live,
to teach,
and most of all to love,
so that others will see you in my life. Amen.

Excerpt from

DEVOTIONS FOR COUPLES

Loving Each Other

Love is patient and kind. Love is not jealous or boastful or proud. (1 Corinthians 13:4)

Week 1, Day 1

When Shirley and I were dating, her mother made a statement that went something like this: "Some married people are kinder to their friends than they are to each other." Over the years I've thought about those words often and determined it wouldn't apply to us.

Sometimes because we love each other, we tend to take the other for granted. We become more considerate of new relationships because we want to establish them. We already have a loving relationship with our lover and therefore do not show concern.

I've noticed that when many couples are in the dating stage, they're courteous and helpful. I've seen the dashing young fellow carefully open doors for the light of his life. I've often seen those same couples a year after their marriage. He gets out of the car and lets her get out by herself.

One of the things Shirley and I decided when we were dating was that I would continue opening doors for her all through our married life. I also said, "If I forget, I expect you to remind me." I'm still opening doors for Shirley because it's my way of saying I care about her and want to do little things for her.

True lovers constantly find ways to show they appreciate each other and to affirm the relationship they have.

True lovers enjoy each other. They do things together, whether it's working, participating in sports, or attending plays and concerts. They share common interests.

True lovers respect each other. They may disagree, but they allow for differences of opinion. When we really love another person, we don't pressure him or her to act contrary to his or her values.

We had a woman in our church who was very talented musically. She once said that people had appreciated her talent for years, but very few had appreciated her as a person. She needed affirmation as a human being and not just recognition of her abilities.

Lovers care by being sensitive to each other's hopes, fears, aspirations, dreams, and plans. The Apostle John writes, "Beloved, let us love one another." "Beloved" could be read as "dear friends," as it is in some translations. He's saying, "As friends, let's love one another." Lovers respect, love, and cherish each other, not only for today but throughout their lives.

Lord God, teach us the full dimensions of love as we discover more about each other and discover more about you. Amen.

Available Love

... For God has said, "I will never fail you. I will never abandon you." (Hebrews 13:5)

Week 1, Day 2

I was involved in an automobile accident four years ago. A man in another car ran through a red light and hit me. My car was severely damaged, and I did not have another vehicle. Several friends told me how sorry they were about my situation. Many of them added something like "If there's anything we can do…." One friend, Bob, never made such a statement. He heard about the accident, called, and said, "For a few days we can get by with one car. We'd like to lend you our second car." Bob's love was available to me.

Often we want to spend time with our friends, but only at our convenience. There are times when we wish to be alone and resent the intrusion of other people and their problems. We like to choose our availability.

Yet true love is available at all times. That doesn't mean I always feel loving, or that I always feel good about being disturbed. But if I really love you I am available to you.

True lovers make themselves available to each other. Available to listen, to talk, to touch, to hold. Available lovers echo the words from Hebrews, "I will never forsake you."

We understand that promise because Jesus Christ gives us the perfect model. God says he will never leave us, and that he will never fail us in any way. True lovers work at imitating that ideal.

Faithful Lord, as we appreciate your availability, may we learn always to be available to each other. Amen.

About the Author

New York Times bestselling author Cecil (Cec) Murphey has written or co-written more than 135 books, including the bestsellers *90 Minutes in Heaven* (with Don Piper) and *Gifted Hands: The Ben Carson Story* (with Dr. Ben Carson). His books have sold in the millions and have brought hope and encouragement to countless people around the world.

Visit his website at www.CecilMurphey.com and follow him on Twitter at www.Twitter.com/CecMurphey.

www.ingramcontent.com/pod-product-compliance
Lightning Source LLC
Chambersburg PA
CBHW051646040426
42446CB00009B/995